P9-DBY-004

PENGUIN BOOKS

NOT QUITE NOT WHITE

Sharmila Sen grew up in Calcutta, India, and immigrated to the United States when she was twelve. She was educated in the public schools of Cambridge, Massachusetts, and received her AB from Harvard and her PhD from Yale in English literature. As an assistant professor at Harvard she taught courses on literature from Africa, Asia, and the Caribbean for seven years. Currently, she is executive editor-at-large at Harvard University Press. Sharmila has lived and worked in India, Pakistan, and Bangladesh. She has lectured around the world on postcolonial literature and culture and published essays on racism and immigration. Sharmila resides in Cambridge, Massachusetts, with her architect husband and their three children.

NOT QUITE NOT WHITE

LOSING AND FINDING RACE IN AMERICA

• • •

Sharmila Sen

PENGUIN BOOKS

PENGUIN BOOKS

An imprint of Penguin Random House LLC
375 Hudson Street
New York, New York 10014
penguinrandomhouse.com

LIBRARY OF CONGRESS CATALOGING-IN-PUBLICATION DATA
Names: Sen, Sharmila, author.
Title: Not quite not white : losing and finding race
in America / Sharmila Sen.
Description: New York, New York : Penguin Books, 2018.
Identifiers: LCCN 2017031011 (print) | LCCN 2017032252 (ebook) | ISBN
9781524705121 (ebook) | ISBN 9780143131380
Subjects: LCSH: Sen, Sharmila, author. | South Asian Americans—Biography. |
South Asian Americans—Social conditions. | South Asian Americans—Ethnic
identity. | South Asian Americans—History. | Racism—United States. |
Group identity—United States. | United States—Race relations.
Classification: LCC E184.S69 (ebook) | LCC E184.S69 S46 2018 (print) |
DDC 305.800973—dc23
LC record available at https://lccn.loc.gov/2017031011

Printed in the United States of America
1 3 5 7 9 10 8 6 4 2

Set in Sabon LT Std • Designed by Elke Sigal

For Ishani, Milan, and Kabir

CONTENTS

Preface

The Mask That Grins

When I was in graduate school at Yale University over twenty years ago, I once asked a friend of mine why everyone always gravitated toward us two at student parties. My friend was one of the few black doctoral candidates in the university at the time. Finding ourselves to be the only minority students in a great many of the seminars we attended, we often joked with each other privately about race and identity as a way of blowing off some steam. I recollect that particular conversation—words whispered over plastic cups in a crowded room—well. With each passing year, our playful exchange has taken on Technicolor oracular tones in my mind:

I hear my friend say: "Sharmila, do I really have to

explain why everyone comes and hangs out with us at parties? Because we are fun. Because we smile and laugh so much."

"Why do we smile so much?" I ask him. "My cheeks hurt from smiling so much and I cannot keep it up."

"We smile," he tells me, "because it is the only face we can show. If we stop smiling, they will see how angry we are. And no one likes an angry black man." *Or an angry brown woman,* I add, silently editing our conversation. "But I think you know this already," he continues, "and so you smile wide and crack all those jokes."

At the end of the nineteenth century, the African American poet Paul Laurence Dunbar wrote,

> We wear the mask that grins and lies,
> It hides our cheeks and shades our eyes

In the early decades of the twenty-first century, I know that if I stop grinning, I will frighten others with my anger. Anger is the useless emotion of people with grievances. Civilized people, superior people, capable people manage anger through reason, televised town hall meetings, logic gates, strategic planning, branding exercises, op-eds, and fireside chats with tea and sherry.

In the universities of America today there are angry students who say that when people of paler complexions use pigments to darken their faces and redden their lips for

Halloween, when people with blond straight hair wear dark curly wigs in order to dress as a rapper, they are insulting black people. "Don't curb our freedom and be a killjoy who doesn't understand that Halloween is about experimentation," say their opponents. "Children, do you want adults to tell you how to dress? Do you want to whine about microaggressions and institutionalized racism? Remember, out there in the real world, outside college, no one will give you trigger warnings in a boardroom meeting." Those who think angry students of color are pampered minorities continue, "Institutionalized racism is a figment of your imagination. This is the reign of emancipation. Jim Crow is a chapter in the history books. The empire has folded up its flags and bid farewell to the natives. Stop complaining, pull up your pants, and learn to have a little fun. We cannot go around changing names of buildings just because the name happens to belong to a white man who owned slaves. Think of all the good qualities the slave owner had. Think of all the wondrous things he did for this country."

"What's wrong with a little racial ventriloquism? Race is just performance. Race is a metaphor. Race is a biological fiction. Let us perform our identities." (These are the graduate-school-educated voices of America.) "What's wrong with having a little fun?" (These are teenage voices in America.) "Parading in blackface is our cultural heritage. We will fight to protect our heritage." (That is Dutch people parading as *Zwarte Piet*, or Black Pete, on Saint Nicholas's Day.) These voices, I wager, are mostly white.

Why do blackface and brownface bother me? Because I have been wearing whiteface for so long. Because my Halloween never ends. The tricks and the treats are not toilet paper and cheap candy. The truth is that the opposite of blackface is not whiteface. Blackface is jolly, makes fun of others, is entertainment, is a game you get to play when you are already the winner. Whiteface is sad, demeans me, is deadly serious, is a game we play when we know we are on the losing team.

Blackface makes me angry because whiteface is not its opposite. And anger is no longer a heroic emotion. The age of Achilles is over. Gods and heroes no longer rage as the topless towers of Ilium burn. Now anger is a Third World emotion. Anger is a militant black. Anger is a shrill woman. Anger is a *jihadi*. Because we know this, many of us also hide our anger behind elaborate masks of comedy.

At Yale, I learned that all binaries are false. That race is a biological lie. That the colonizer never fully dominates. That the colonized are never fully subjugated. That there are things called Ambiguity, Ambivalence, Aporia. And those were just the A words. There were also Hybridities, Problematics, and we had to Complicate Things. Outside class, there were people whose cheeks hurt from smiling because they feared the consequences of revealing their anger. Perhaps because we perfected our smiles, students young enough to be my daughters and sons have to be seen raging on YouTube.

Almost twenty years after I graduated from Yale with a PhD, in the spring of 2016 I was invited to speak to graduate students at my alma mater. My hosts asked me to speak on racism on campus and the experience of non-white alumni in the workplace. There are many ways of comporting oneself at such an event—in each version I could emerge as the triumphant heroine of my own story. I could speak of hard work and the high road, and end on an upbeat note. I could speak more clinically, do a Produnova vault across critical race theory, and nail my landing with a virtuoso flourish that would demonstrate that there is no such thing as race after all. I could be somber and tragic, listing all the slings and arrows borne patiently since graduation. I could be the comedienne of color who outruns and outguns racism with her swift wit.

We were scheduled to meet on the third floor of Linsly-Chittenden Hall on Old Campus, in a classroom where nearly all my graduate seminars used to meet. When I walked into that room, I knew that none of the story lines were right for the occasion. If I could not bring myself to tell the truth in the very room where I was educated, then what was the value of the diploma written in Latin that Yale once gave me? I cannot play the role of the photogenic minority alumna who has managed some small amount of professional success. I cannot be the poster girl for diversity in a glossy magazine targeted at wealthy donors. So, I told them that as a young woman I once sat in that very room and smiled until my cheeks hurt. I confessed that I entertained classmates with elaborate masks of comedy. I said that I wish I had the courage to be as angry as the young people who are protesting institutional racism in campuses all over the country right now.

· · ·

These young people are the Angry Young Men of a new century. In the last century, the Angry Young Men were mostly young white men, working class and middle class. The British playwright John Osborne immortalized the type in his 1956 play *Look Back in Anger*. There is a famous scene in that play when a young woman named Alison tells her father that he is hurt because everything has changed, and her husband is hurt because everything is the same. Alison's father, Colonel Redfern, is a retired British Army officer who'd served in India. Her husband, Jimmy Porter, is a disaffected working-class man who spends a great deal of time berating his wife. The play is set in postwar London during the twilight years of the British Empire. Colonel Redfern, an upper-class military man, is hurt—I would use the word "angry"—because the old days of Britannia's global power have come to an end in the aftermath of World War II. Jimmy Porter is angry because nothing has changed since the prewar days. The old social hierarchies still hold him down, while dark newcomers appear on the horizon—immigrants from places like Jamaica and Nigeria and Pakistan and India—jostling for jobs alongside native-born whites.

I have very little in common with these angry British men—the old one and the young one. I was born in India, the jewel that once sparkled in the British crown. My people are the immigrants who darkened the streets of Jimmy Porter's postwar Britain, filling its labor vacuum. Yet, Alison's words have always resonated deeply with me. I have been both Colonel Redfern and Jimmy Porter. I have been angry because everything has changed. I have been angry because nothing has changed.

When the Angry Young Man is white, male, and British, he is a cultural icon, an artistic rendering of midcentury Britain's social and cultural struggle. When the play was adapted for a film version, Richard Burton played the role of Jimmy Porter. Eventually, the Angry Young Man traveled to other countries. Wherever he went, he was a member of the dominant culture who felt cheated out of his rightful place in society. Can the Angry Young Man be black? Or a woman? Or an immigrant? I think not. There are other words we use for angry blacks, angry women, and angry immigrants. Those creatures are threatening, unnatural, ungrateful, a problem. Because I know this, I have spent many decades carefully arranging my words, my gestures, my clothes, and my surroundings so that I do not appear threatening, unnatural, or ungrateful. I did not want to be the kind of problem who does not receive good grades in school, or glowing letters of recommendation, or college acceptance letters. I did not want to be perceived as the ungrateful immigrant who does not pass her naturalization examination, the unnatural woman who is never promoted at work or paid a salary equal to that of her white male counterparts. I feared being perceived as the threatening creature who might be detained longer by customs and immigration officers, and even worse, whose children might be seen as threats and problems as well. I envy Colonel Redfern and Jimmy Porter—white men can openly rage against everything changing *and* against nothing changing. I envy them, for their rage is not arrested.

When I arrived in the United States as a young immigrant in 1982, everything changed for me. The Colonel Redfern in me raged against the change, for it made me a minority, marked by race. After I arrived in the United States, I acted as a model new immigrant. I changed my accent, my food habits, my dress, and eventually my citizenship. Yet, I fear little has changed. This angers the Jimmy Porter in me. I am angry when a colleague tells me I gained admission into universities only because I am a minority. I am angry when an adviser tells me that I have to learn six languages in order to pass a three-language requirement in graduate school. I am angry when a coworker tells me I am an affirmative action hire who does not deserve her position in the office. I am angry when people inevitably assume my white male assistant is my boss. I am angry at myself for feigning ignorance, hiding my accomplishments, softening the sharp edges of my arguments, pretending to lack conviction, throwing the game so I can remain the token minority who brings pleasant diversity to a white workplace. I am angry at myself for hushing my native-born son when he complains that a teacher systematically confuses the names of all the brown boys in class. Jimmy Porter went on to become an archetype. Do I dare reclaim his anger?

· · ·

Anger, everyone tells me, is unbecoming. When I was a child in Calcutta, the Bengali society in which I was brought up made it clear that anger was inappropriate in a young woman. English words such as "compromise" and "adjustment" were frequently mentioned—even in Bengali conversations—when talking to a girl whose marriage was to be arranged to a suitable boy. We lived in independent India of the 1970s. Middle-class parents in Calcutta sent their girls to convent schools, expecting them to learn mathematics, history, geography, physics, chemistry, biology, and literature in Bengali and English, as well as knitting, needlework, and cooking. As a young girl, I had an ideal vision of myself as an adult: I am wearing a pale pink chiffon sari with a sleeveless, scoop-neck blouse. I have stylish platform heels (it was the 1970s after all). My glossy black hair is long enough to reach my waist. My eyebrows are plucked thin. A tasteful string of pearls floats around my neck. My English is fluent and classy. My Bengali is cultured and soft. My penmanship is flawless. My cross-stitch embroidery work is spectacular. My hemstitch is invisible. My buttonhole stitch is delicate and uniform. I can cook four kinds of cuisine—Bengali, Mughlai, Chinese, and Continental—without breaking a sweat. My complexion is light and untouched by the sun. This, I imagined, was the ideal woman. No one described her to me. I pieced her together from novels, magazines, films, radio programs, songs, jokes, and the subtle looks of approval and disdain I spied in the eyes of adults.

The ideal modern Bengali woman of my vision was never angry. That would be coarse and beneath our station. Anger was associated with the working class, with trade union leaders, with minorities, with the uneducated and the poor, with the weak and the uncivilized. And anger was decidedly unfeminine. If I had read Virginia Woolf at that age, I would have known that my ideal modern Bengali had an older sister in Victorian England. She was called the Angel in the House. When I was a freshman in college, I was assigned to read Virginia Woolf's send-up of the Angel in a literature class. I recognized her immediately as the woman I once idealized. Woolf said the Angel in the House was "intensely sympathetic," "immensely charming," and "utterly unselfish," and she "sacrificed herself daily." "If there was chicken, she took the leg; if there was a draught she sat in it." I read this one line repeatedly because it described with comic precision so many women I knew while I was growing up. I only needed to rearrange Woolf's English words ever so slightly for them to fit my Bengali universe perfectly. In damp and chilly London, it is a sacrifice to sit in a drafty room. In tropical Calcutta, the Angel sits in the corner where the cool easterly breeze never blows. Since chicken appears less frequently in our rice-and-fish cuisine, the Bengali Angel takes the cartilaginous tail end of the fish, leaving the delicacy of the fish head or the fleshy fillets for the men. She sits down for her meals after the men have their fill and considers it a badge of honor to eat off her husband's dirty plate.

I had another secret ambition as a young girl. I wanted to be the prime minister of the nation. I did not see these two dreams—being the chiffon-sari-wearing, fishtail-eating Bengali woman and being the political leader of the nation—as contradictory. Indira Gandhi was the prime minister of India when I was a young girl. Unlike American girls, I did not have to wait until the twenty-first century for the political glass ceiling to be cracked. If Mrs. Gandhi could run the country in her elegant cotton saris, we young girls could easily see ourselves running for elections, making laws, and giving speeches from Delhi's Red Fort on Independence Day.

As it turned out, I never did grow my hair long or own a pink chiffon sari or run for public office. And fish tails never appealed to me.

During the 1970s, I was surrounded by fierce and powerful women of another variety. The beautiful goddess Durga—with ten arms, four children, three eyes, and one blue husband—rides her lion ferociously through my childhood years. She slays demons that no male god can defeat. We await her visit to her earthly home each autumn for five fragrant days when the coral-tipped, white *sheuli* flowers bloom. In Bengali, we call those five sacred days *shashthi, shaptami, ashtami, navami,* and *dashami.* After Durga leaves us and returns to the realm of the gods, Kali arrives. The goddess Kali is ever present in Bengali life. She is no simple mother goddess. She is murderous in her rage. Yet, we adore her as our mother and daughter. Kali, for me, is the closest equivalent to the angry god of the Hebrew Bible. She is rather different, of course, from the deity Moses encountered on Mount Sinai. Kali is a dark-skinned goddess, naked, usually depicted with a skirt of severed hands, a necklace of skulls, hair flowing in black waves. Her anger is a necessary part of life. Destruction can never be separated from creation and preservation. There is, however, a small catch. Even destruction has to be destroyed. Kali is depicted in Bengal with her red tongue lolling, frozen in the moment when she steps on the prone body of her husband, Shiva. She is the personification of anger arrested.

Goddesses were not the only women allowed a little bit of rage in my adolescent universe. Epic heroines could rage freely as well. Draupadi, the wife of the five Pandava brothers in the Indian epic the *Mahabharata*, always appealed to me more than the long-suffering Sita in the *Ramayana*. Sita might have walked through fire to appease her husband Ram's insecurity, but Draupadi speaks up when her husband stupidly loses a game of dice and makes her the property of his cousins. She does not accept her degradation silently. She leaves her hair undone and announces that she will tie it up only after she has washed it in the blood of her tormentor. Draupadi, as every little girl who pays attention to the *Mahabharata* knows, holds on to a grudge, refuses to take the high road of forgiveness, and exacts her revenge. When the great war is over in the *Mahabharata*, Draupadi finally gets to wash her hair in her enemy's blood. She was no Angel in the House.

Right around the time I started reading the *Mahabharata* in various Bengali editions prepared for teenagers, I also discovered Louisa May Alcott's nineteenth-century classic *Little Women*, written for children of a different country, of a different era. The *Mahabharata* offered in print a world with which I was already acquainted. When my mother fed me lunch, when my aunt combed the tangles out of my wet hair, when my grandmother rubbed Jabakusum hair oil into my scalp, they told me stories from the *Mahabharata* to distract, educate, and entertain. If there was a time in my life when I did not know that Bhima defeats Duryodhona or that Karna is Kunti's first-born son, I do not recall that time. American children's books, in contrast, transported me to an unknown terrain through the printed page. When I read the Indian epics, printed words gave shape to emotions, smells, and sights already familiar. When I read American or British books, the words on the page made the unfamiliar recognizable. As a result, when I immigrated to Jo's New England later in my life, I saw the landscape, tasted the food, and felt the chill on my skin first through Alcott's words. As Prospero teaches Caliban to name the sun and the moon in *The Tempest*, Alcott gave me the first words to name things in my new home. The dove-colored book Marmee gave Beth revealed a New England shade that no Pantone color will ever capture.

Jo March's temper fascinated me. Her mother, Marmee, was no stranger to anger herself. Mr. March and Professor Bhaer trained their wives to control that temper. As much as I loved reading about Meg, Jo, Beth, Amy, and Laurie, I always disliked the pedantic, priggish side of the novel.

When I first read Louisa May Alcott's stories, I had only the vaguest sense of their context. Unburdened by knowledge of New England, the American Civil War, or nineteenth-century American society, my adolescent imagination relocated the March family to the same magical place outside of time where the Pandavas and the Kauravas, or Ram and Sita, or Ali Baba and Sinbad resided. In India, I had read *Little Women* as an allegory—much like John

Bunyan's *The Pilgrim's Progress*, the book the girls receive as a Christmas gift from their mother at the beginning of the story. When the specific is unknown to us, most of us are tempted to reach for the general. Novels about "foreign lands" are often read as full-blown national allegories by literary critics. The four girls, their parents, their home, their travails were a fuzzy stand-in for *all* of America.

Once I understood why the Civil War was being fought, I came to see that the March family represented only one part of America—white, northeastern, Anglo-Saxon, Protestant. What is more, I started to perceive that the book was written from a very specific perspective as well. These little women no more represented all girls in the United States of that era than the narrator represented all possible narrative voices. The first part of the novel we now call *Little Women* was published in the United States in 1868, three years after the end of the Civil War, and five years after President Lincoln's Emancipation Proclamation declared "all persons held as slaves" to be "forever free." As a young girl living in independent India, I was unaware that the America in which the March sisters lived withheld freedom and full citizenship from so many of its inhabitants because of their race. Today, I try to imagine an all-black-cast production of *Little Women*. How would a black Jo fare in the United States during the 1860s? Or a Hispanic Jo? Or an Indian Jo? Or a Chinese Jo? How would Jo write her story if she was not white? How would she write her story if she was one of the Hummels, a first-generation immigrant?

. . .

In 1982, a little over half a million legal immigrants entered the United States. The numbers are surely much greater if we include the undocumented in this rough tally. Some stayed and flourished. Some left after a while. Others fared poorly and were disappointed. Many of their descendants are American citizens now. I arrived in the United States during the second week of August in 1982. I was nearly twelve and accompanied by my parents when we landed in Boston's Logan International Airport. Before arriving in Boston, I had never left Asia, or even traveled beyond the borders of India. That year, the Immigration and Naturalization Service provided us aliens with many forms, a Social Security number, and occasionally a Resident Alien card. I received a bonus gift from the INS that year. I got race.

The uniquely American concept of race that I inherited upon arrival was shaped by two symmetrical genres of early American writing—the captivity narrative and the slave narrative. Both genres racialize religion and religionize race. In the last couple of decades another type of race narrative has appeared on the horizon—the clash of civilizations theory. This theory has made explicit the implicit intertwining of race and religion in the West since the Protestant Reformation. If you listen closely to American race talk today, you will hear the echoes of old slave narratives and captivity narratives; and you will also discern shades of the idea that Islam and Christianity, much like the Rebel Alliance and the Galactic Empire, are locked in perpetual enmity.

The election of the forty-fourth president of the United States led some to declare that race was a place best glimpsed through the rearview mirror. The election of our forty-fifth president cautions us that the postracial world, should we wish to enter it, remains a mirage shimmering on the horizon, redlined and gerrymandered, walled and banned. Even though race is largely understood as a biological fiction by scientists, even though many American writers have questioned the fact of whiteness, racism is as much a social reality for my generation as I suspect it will continue to be for my children's generation.

I am a Hindu, with no cross or crescent, no church or mosque, no covenant with one true god, no commitment to the doctrine of *sola scriptura*. There is no exact equivalent for "religion" or "race" in my mother tongue. Multiple languages and writing systems—Bengali, Hindi, English— have formed the ideas, including that of race and religion, that I carry within me. What happens when race is not inherited at birth, but acquired, even chosen, later in life? What happens when you get race after you arrive as an immigrant to the United States? Throughout this book I will use the odd formulation of getting race because I want to show you how I once perceived race as an alien object, a thing outside myself, a disease. I got race the way people get chicken pox. I also got race as one gets a pair of shoes or a cell phone. It was something new, something to be tried on for size, something to be used to communicate with others. In another register, I finally got race, in the idiomatic American sense of fully comprehending something. *You get what I'm saying? Yeah, I get you.*

While most native-born American authors write about race—angrily, passionately, elegiacally, tersely—as something they did not really choose but had forced upon them since birth, I will write about race as something once alien to my universe and later naturalized. Looking back to 1982, I now realize that race was the immigrant and I was the homeland where it came to rest. Instead of rejecting it as I once did—most of my Indian intellectual friends would consider it a silly American affectation to identify as a "person of color" and prefer instead to think in terms of social class, of majority and minority religions, of imperialists and subalterns—I eventually chose to keep race, despite its unlovely history, its elusive and fictional nature. It is not the accent I carefully picked up from watching television after school, or the way I learned to talk about books at Ivy League universities, or the way I copied the food and drink habits of those around me, or even the way I learned to make the right mistakes in English (because only ESL speakers use perfectly starched and ironed English), but getting race that made me fully American.

In order to tell this story, I must steal some ire from the gods and epic heroes. Let Draupadi hold her grudge as the war of Kurukshetra rages. Let Durga slay the demon Mahishasura this autumn and every autumn to come. Let Kali rage, unchecked by Shiva. In their cozy American parlors, let Marmee and Jo not be hushed by Mr. March and Professor Bhaer. In Bloomsbury, London, let the Angel in the House breathe her last once more. Let Achilles rage outside the walls of Troy so a new story may be plotted.

This book is an immigrant's pagan confession, an assimilationist's tongue-in-cheek DIY manual for whiteface performance, and the story of an American's long journey into the heart of Not Whiteness.

NOT QUITE
NOT WHITE

Chapter One

• • •

Enter the Dragon

I had never seen a black man in person until I was twelve years old. If I search my memory hard enough, I can see a few faded newspaper photographs of West Indian cricketers in the *Statesman*. I can see dark-skinned Africans within the panels of my beloved *Phantom* comics. There are faint recollections of black James Bond villains in *Live and Let Die*. If I squint even more, I can remember the evening when we crowded into our neighbor's drawing room, watching Pelé on a black-and-white television set, the first procured in our middle-class neighborhood. The first flesh-and-blood black man I saw was standing outside the entrance to the U.S. consulate in Calcutta, which is located on a street named after Ho Chi Minh. At the entrance to the consulate where Ma, Baba, and I had gone for our visa interviews, I saw two men in spotless uniforms. One was the whitest, blondest man I had ever seen in real life; the other was the darkest black.

The consulate smelled like America in my childish imagination. The air-conditioned halls, the modern plastic and metal furniture, a water cooler from which I eagerly poured myself some water even though I was not thirsty. I breathed in the scent of wealth in there. It felt like newness on my skin. Everything was hushed, ordered, brightly lit. Not like my own loud, bustling city. Even the local Indian staff seemed to behave as if they were actually living in America.

I stood at the entrance of the U.S. consulate in Calcutta in 1982. In 1965, American immigration laws had been rewritten to allow for a greater number of non-Europeans to enter the country. Not only were Indians and other Asians considered unwanted newcomers before 1965, even naturalization—the process by which a foreign-born immigrant becomes a U.S. citizen—was disallowed for most who were not white until the 1950s. I knew little of this history when I entered the consulate with my parents. I did not even know I had something called race. Race as a category had not been part of the Indian census since 1951. I was about to move to a nation where nearly every official form had a section in which I would be offered an array of racial categories and expected to pick one.

In 1982, as it happens, it was not clear which race should be affixed to my person. Since the number of Indian immigrants was fairly insignificant in the United States until the latter part of the twentieth century, the census barely took notice of us. At the time of the first U.S. census in 1790, there were essentially three races acknowledged by the government—white, black, and Indian. My kind of Indians, the ones from the subcontinent, however, fell into none of these categories. No matter how mysterious our race, we were not considered white during most of the nineteenth and twentieth centuries by the American courts. In 1970, the U.S. Census Bureau declared people from India to be legally white. A decade later, in 1980, we were officially reclassified as Asian by the government, at the insistence of Indian immigrant groups who believed that the new classification would afford us greater affirmative action benefits. Yet, what was to be done with the decision to make Indians white only a decade earlier? What would happen to those white Indians? "Self-reporting" was the Solomonic solution to this problem. In order to satisfy the demands of the diverse Indian community, after nearly a century of shuffling people from the Indian subcontinent from one racial category to another, the U.S. census had finally thrown up its hands in despair and asked us to "self-report" our race. In the 1990 U.S. census, of the native-born population with origins in the Indian subcontinent, nearly a quarter reported themselves to be white, a tiny minority (5 percent) reported themselves to be black, and the vast majority chose to report their race using terms that pertain to South Asia.

Such an astounding array of choices was not always available to people from India who found themselves in the United States a century ago. If Ma, Baba, and I could have embarked on a time machine and arrived in the country eight decades earlier, we would have found ourselves in a different situation. If I had immigrated in 1909, I would have been labeled "probably not white," but a year later—when the U.S. courts decided to change their opinion on the matter—I would have been "white." If I was Sadar Bhagwab Singh in 1917, or Akhay Kumar Mozumdar in 1919, or Bhagat Singh Thind in 1923, I would have been "not white." Naturalization in the United States was reserved mostly for whites between 1790 and the middle of the twentieth century. Non-white immigrants could not become naturalized and partake of the rights reserved for U.S. citizens. Indians were not allowed to become naturalized citizens until the 1940s. They could, however, toil in American factories and fields, offices and streets. So Indian men such as Singh, Mozumdar, and Thind kept trying in vain to prove they were white in order to become naturalized citizens. But what actually made a person "white"? Could you be both "Caucasian" and "non-white"? As Singh, Mozumdar, and Thind all found out, yes, you could be Caucasian and also Not White. The courts ruled repeatedly in those early decades of the twentieth century that naturalization was for "whites" only, and some "Caucasians" were not truly "white" enough to qualify.

That the two words—Caucasian and white—are used interchangeably today would come as a bittersweet surprise to all who were caught in the deep chasm between those labels a century ago. Yet, that is exactly the chasm in which people from the Indian subcontinent, an area that is second only to Africa in its genetic and linguistic diversity, were placed by the U.S. courts. In those early years of the twentieth century, miscegenation laws could have prevented me from marrying a white American in states such as South Carolina, Georgia, and Virginia. The former governor of South Carolina and the current U.S. ambassador to the United Nations, Nikki Haley, identifies herself as "white" on her voter registration card. Of course, according to the laws of this country, Haley can legally self-report her race any way she pleases. The former governor of South Carolina was born Nimrata Nikki Randhawa, daughter of Punjabi Sikh immigrants from India, and the racial category she chooses for herself tells a complex story of the state where the first shots of the Civil War were fired, and where even today West African–inflected Gullah culture (brought by black slaves) does not easily mix with white French Huguenot culture (brought by white slave owners).

A hundred years ago Indians immigrated to the United States in very small numbers. They were mostly agricultural workers who traversed the networks of the British Empire, sailors who stayed behind in American ports, or Hindu holy men who were invited to lecture in cities such as New York and Chicago. The Immigration Act of 1917 placed India squarely within the Asiatic Barred Zone, an area from which immigrants were not allowed to legally enter the United States. This zone would not be legally un-barred until 1946.

Contemporary racial labels used in everyday American parlance are an odd amalgamation of the geographic (Asian), the linguistic (Hispanic), and the pseudo-biological (black, white). The rise of Islamophobia threatens to racialize Islam and conflates race with religion. This, however, is not a new phenomenon in American history. Early-twentieth-century America was still in the old habit of seeing Jews as "Hebrews"—as much a racial label as a religious one. It also happened that many Jews themselves preferred this system—until the murderous actions of the Nazis in Europe—because Judaism cannot be folded neatly into the box we call "reli-gion" today, a box whose dimensions are largely of Protes-tant specifications. Similarly, "Hindoo" was as much a racial label as a religion in early-twentieth-century America. Today what is considered my religious background might have been seen as my racial identity had I arrived in America at the beginning of the last century.

The Immigration and Nationality Act of 1965, signed by Lyndon B. Johnson, changed the quota system that restricted non-European immigrants from coming to the United States. People like me were going to become a bit more common on American soil. Hindoo, Asiatic, Caucasian, non-white, brown, Asian, South Asian. During the era of self-reporting in the early 1980s, I was a young girl faced with a plethora of racial categories based on a wild mash-up of genetics, linguistics, theology, and geography, who landed in Boston on August 11, 1982. The entry date is marked on my first passport.

I carried an Indian passport back then. Navy blue with thick cardboard covers. I received that passport in December 1979. On page four, there is a line printed in minuscule letters: "Countries for which this Passport is valid." Below it a stamp, in purplish blue ink, slightly tilted, partly smudged, is still vividly legible after nearly forty years. It says (first in Hindi): *"sabhi desh dakshin afrika aur rodeshiya ko chhorkar*—ALL COUNTRIES Except Republic of South Africa and Colony of Rhodesia."

Before immigrating to the United States, I had never left India. My 1979 passport was an aspirational possession. Yet, I was already becoming aware of certain countries that were forbidden to me. My parents explained that India did not allow me to travel to South Africa or Rhodesia because of something called apartheid. There existed places where people like us had gone as coolie labor, as merchants and traders, and even as lawyers (the young Mahatma Gandhi practiced law in Pretoria in the 1890s), during the time of the British. But white people did not treat brown and black people fairly and each group had to live apart. Unlike my forebears who had borne the "malodorousness of subjecthood" for two centuries—as the Indian political scientist Niraja Jayal once wrote—I was fragrant with citizenship and protected by the laws of my nation. And those laws prevented me from going to Rhodesia and South Africa, places where complex designations such as black, colored, Indian, and white would determine where I could live, where I could go to school, and who I could marry. But in the late 1970s, when I received my passport, I barely grasped what apartheid really meant.

Caucasian but Not White. Not White and Not Black. Minority. Non-Christian. Person of Color. South Asian. I never thought of myself as any of these things before the autumn of 1982. I had grown up back in Calcutta with an entirely different set of extended labels for putting people into boxes. What language do you speak? Which gods do you worship? Which caste do you belong to? Are you part of the *bhadralok* (the Bengali word for the bourgeoisie)? Do you eat with relish the flesh of animals, fowl, fish, and crustaceans? Do you eat beef? Or do you eat only plants and grains? "Veg" and "Non-veg" in India are almost as evocative and important as "black" and "white" in America. We can detect a person's religion, caste, and ethnic group from the foods they eat and the foods they shun. Every society invents ways of partitioning themselves and methods of reading the hidden signs displayed by those who wish to cheat the rules. A person of a lower caste might want to pass as a Brahmin; a Muslim might want to pretend to be a Hindu when caught in the middle of a riot; a Hindu might pose as a Muslim to gain entry to a restricted space. We were taught to be vigilant about such trespassers. An Indian's surname holds a multitude of information about her. In India, if you know my surname is Sen, you already know which language I speak as my mother tongue, my caste, the religious holidays I celebrate, my likely economic class, my literacy status, whether I am vegetarian, the birth, wedding, and funeral rites I might have. Conversely, a last name that holds very little information is suspect. What is this person trying to hide? The way one pronounces a certain word, the way a woman drapes her *dupatta* over her head, how her nose is pierced, whether a man's foreskin is intact or circumcised, whether a little boy has a red thread around his wrist or a *tabeez*, an amulet, around his neck signifies so many things in India. In some cases, it can mean the difference between being killed by a mob during a communal riot and being pulled into safety. We had all these distinguishing labels. But race we did not have.

· · ·

I grew up in India for the first twelve years of my life without race. After ruling us for two centuries, the British had departed in 1947. The India of my childhood was a place marked by what economists call "capital flight." These were years preceding the arrival of economic liberalization. Before the Internet and cheap cell phones, our knowledge of

the United States was channeled largely by a few Hollywood movies, occasional headlines in the newspapers, magazines such as *Life* and *Reader's Digest*, and hand-me-down
clothing brought back by relatives who had immigrated to
the West. Television had not fully arrived in India during
the first half of the 1970s. We tried halfheartedly to imitate
American fashion, eat American fast food, or listen to
American popular music. Still, we were always a few years
behind on the trends. Of course, we were also happy with
our own popular culture. We watched Hindi films made in
Bombay, hummed along to the songs aired on All India
Radio, and ate delicious street foods such as *phuchka* and
jhalmuri without missing global chains such as KFC or Mc-
Donald's. Our drinking water was procured daily from the
neighborhood tube well. Ma, Baba, and I each had our own
official ration cards. These rations cards were used for purchasing government-subsidized basic commodities—rice,
flour, sugar—which we used to complement our groceries
from the local bazaars. I had never seen a mall or a supermarket before I came to the United States. Ma and Baba did
not own a telephone, a washing machine, a television, a
cassette player, a car, or a credit card until we emigrated.
Our sole mode of personal transportation was a blue Lambretta scooter purchased by Baba in the mid-1970s. When
Baba was not there to take us around on the scooter,
hand-pulled rickshaws, red double-decker buses, trams, and

the occasional taxi were the usual ways we navigated the sprawling metropolis that was Calcutta.

We vaguely understood ourselves to be Not White because our grandparents and parents still remembered a time when white Europeans ruled us. The Indian notion of Not Whiteness was shaped more by nationalism than by race talk. The subcontinental obsession with skin color cannot be explained solely through the American grammar of racism. In a subcontinent where melanin can appear in wildly differing quantities among family members, the lightness or darkness of one's skin cannot easily be used to mark rigid racial boundaries. Yet, the preference for paler skin was clear to all in Calcutta. Girls with "fair" skin were supposed to fare better than those with "wheatish" or "dark" skin when marriages were to be arranged. I grew up reading numerous sentimental tearjerkers about sisters whose fates were determined by their complexions—the fair one always married well and the dark one was forever shunned by all prospective bridegrooms. Rabindranath Tagore's famous lyric about the beauty of the black-skinned woman's dark doe eyes was quoted often in literary families, marked by the same self-righteousness with which well-off Americans buy fair trade coffee beans. Still, I never came across a matrimonial advertisement in any newspaper that boasted of a dark-skinned girl's beautiful doe eyes.

I was warned regularly not to darken my own light

complexion by playing too long under the noonday sun. Mothers and grandmothers had numerous homemade concoctions at the ready for keeping my skin pale. A ladleful of cream skimmed from the top of the milk pail, fresh ground turmeric, and sandalwood paste, as well as numerous citrus fruits, flowers, leaves, seeds, and nuts, were our allies in the endless war against the sun's skin-darkening rays. Women walked around Calcutta brandishing colorful umbrellas during the sunniest days lest the "fair" turn into "wheatish" or the "wheatish" into "dark." Some of us had complexions as light as any European, but we knew that an invisible line divided us from the pink-hued Dutch, English, French, and Portuguese. In the comic books of my childhood, the colorists painted the Europeans a homogeneous shade of pale rose and reserved every shade from light beige to dark mahogany to the brightest cerulean blue for Indians. This is how I saw the world as a girl—Europeans were pink. We were not.

It would be a lie of the greatest magnitude if I were to claim that I lived in a society of equals, in a society without barriers, hierarchies, and labels, before I came to the United States. I have already said that I grew up as an elite—a speaker of the dominant language of my state, part of the dominant ethnolinguistic group, and a follower of the majority religion. I was an upper-caste Hindu Bengali. The maternal side of my family were *haute bourgeoisie*, or upper middle class, by virtue of their landowner past. Three generations ago, some of these landowners—called *zamindars* in India—had turned to law, one of the few professions open to Indians under British colonial rule. They trained in law in Britain and returned to India as barristers, dressed in European-style clothes, living in homes furnished with massive Victorian teak furniture. In time, some of these ancestors—men of my great-grandfather's generation—had made the transition from practicing law to agitating for political freedom from British rule. Eighteenth-century American colonies had seen similar professional trajectories from law to revolutionary politics.

On my father's side of the family, our cultural capital outstripped our financial capital. Ours was a family of scholars and intellectuals. In some parts of our home state, West Bengal, the mere mention of my grandfather's name endeared me to total strangers. I did not need to read the French sociologist Pierre Bourdieu's book *Distinction* in order to learn that one can inherit cultural capital just as conveniently as one can inherit property, stocks, jewelry, or money. My paternal grandfather did not leave me a house or a trust fund. But he did give me a slight edge over my peers.

Our school textbooks often included short essays on historical topics written by well-known Bengali intellectuals. One of those essays focused on Rani Lakshmibai of Jhansi, a nineteenth-century Indian queen famous for going to battle against the British who annexed her kingdom. Whenever we read that essay in class, I sat up a little straighter. We were supposed to take pride in our female ancestors who fought British men on the battlefield long before the independence movement was born. My pride, however, was of a pettier sort than grand nationalist sentiments. My grandfather was the author of that essay. Each time I saw his name in print, I felt a secret pride swell inside me. I was the descendant of a man whose writing was part of the official school syllabus. Even though I did not always tell my classmates or my teachers that the author was my grandfather, the knowledge itself was my cloak of protection. It gave me confidence—a bit of smugness even—that I took for granted. This is how elitism works.

• • •

My education in Calcutta began before I turned three. My parents enrolled me in a preschool modeled on the Italian doctor Maria Montessori's theories of education. It was a coeducational school for middle-class children. Most of my classmates were Bengali and the teachers spoke to us in Bengali. We played with blocks, separated white rice from yellow lentils, and began learning the English alphabet phonetically. At that point in my life, I could read "cat" or "bat" or "rat," but I could not really speak or understand any English. When I turned four, I was admitted to a school for girls run by Catholic nuns. Most middle-class parents tried very hard to enroll their children in private schools because state-run schools were considered inferior to even the most mediocre of private schools. In a poor country where jobs are scarce, enrolling one's child into the "right" school by the age of four easily balloons into an existential crisis. I had to be interviewed by a small committee in order to gain admission into this school. But how was an interview to be arranged? That required a form as rare and as precious as diamonds from the Golkonda mines of India. The admissions form for this school was released on a particular day each year. Like many middle-class fathers at schools across the country, Baba stood in a line outside the school building all night to procure the form on the day of its release. Yet, he was not successful. Later, as it happens often in Calcutta, a distant acquaintance who knew someone with a connection to the school administration managed to get us a form. Baba filled out that form. I never laid eyes on it. I was told that it was very difficult to procure the form. Baba had done his part by turning to his network. Now it was my turn.

The interview that followed was entirely my responsibility. I remember every detail of that interview. A nun opened the school gates and took me in. Baba was not allowed inside. Ma had dressed me in a cotton frock and crepe-soled white sandals purchased from Green & Co. in New Market, Calcutta's upscale shopping arcade before the era of malls. My short hair was oiled, parted on the side, and kept off my face with a black metal bobby pin. My neck had been dusted with perfumed talcum powder.

The main trick for passing that interview was to remain calm. The questions themselves were very simple. I am sure four-year-olds are quizzed on far more academically rigorous subjects in India's school admissions process nowadays. In 1974, the nuns were testing me to see if I would burst into tears when separated from my parents and faced with women in strange-looking clothes. Frocked, sandaled, oiled, powdered, and pinned, I was a battle-ready four-year-old Bengali girl. I did not burst into tears. The gray habits and the large crucifixes hanging from their necks did not frighten me. My comprehension of English was tested next. Could a young Bengali girl with no prior English-medium education be able to conduct a rudimentary conversation in English? I have no memory of when I had learned the little bit of English that saw me through that morning. My Montessori school had offered no lessons in conversational English. I spoke Bengali with my family and neighborhood friends. I spoke broken Hindi with our doorman, Hriday Singh, whom I called Darwanji. I understood Hindi from having watched many Hindi movies since I was a toddler and from the near-constant stream of Hindi film music emanating from various transistor radios around the neighborhood. Baba and Ma could speak English. Perhaps I had overheard them speaking with other adults. And they had taken me to see Hollywood films.

The first film I recall watching in a movie theater was Bruce Lee's last film, *Enter the Dragon*. The final fight sequence in a hall of mirrors is perhaps the earliest recollection I have of an entire film sequence. I can see the villain being impaled on a spear and hanging from the mirror even now. A Hong Kong–Hollywood martial arts movie, the last one the legendary Lee would make, might have been responsible for giving me just enough English to pass my first school interview. Bruce Lee died in Hong Kong in July 1973. I did not know that when I looked the nuns straight in the eye and answered the questions they asked me in 1974. I did not know Bruce Lee changed how Asians were depicted in Hollywood movies. I did not even understand he was Asian, just as one day Americans would call me Asian.

"What is your name?"

"My name is Sharmila Sen."

"What is this?"

"A banana."

"Do you know what color it is?"

"Yellow."

"Well done."

That was all. I had managed to answer three questions in English and I had done so without resorting to Bengali. I was admitted into the school. Baba was happy as he walked me home. I had not let him down. Not everyone had managed to gain admission to the school that morning. All around me I saw other girls who were in tears, being led

away by frustrated parents who were scolding them for not
acing the interview. Some of these girls would be admitted
into other English-medium schools. Others would go into a
separate educational track—Bengali-medium. To the list of
labels we use to categorize people in India, let me add one
more—English-medium. Those who are lucky enough to be
educated in English-medium schools usually find more employment opportunities, more economic benefits, more upward mobility, and more cultural capital than those who
attend schools where the medium of instruction is one of the
numerous modern Indian languages. This was true in the
1970s and is even more true in the neoliberal economy of
twenty-first-century India. How else would we become the
world's back office? How else would call centers be staffed?
How else would we send white-collar emigrants who excel
in the STEM professions to the United States?

Having supplied my name, correctly recognized a fruit,
and identified its color, I was on my way to a privileged
English-medium life. Every morning I dressed in a blue
pleated skirt and a white blouse, wore black Mary Janes
with navy socks, and got on a gray school bus. On gym
days I wore white canvas shoes and in the winter I wore a
navy blue cardigan over my blouse. My fellow classmates
and I recited the Lord's Prayer at least four times a day.
Once before the bus reached school, then during morning
assembly, again at dismissal time, and finally when the bus

departed from the school. The majority of us were not Christian. Our nuns were Indian, not European. Only the most elite schools had white European nuns or priests. My family could not afford the fees of such schools.

Miss Solomon was my first teacher. She had a dark brown complexion, bobbed salt-and-pepper hair, and wore Western-style clothes to school. Miss Solomon was an Anglo-Indian. Somewhere in her family tree she had a European ancestor and she was Christian. Anglo-Indians have always occupied a complex position in Indian society. In the nineteenth century, the British derisively referred to biracial men and women as Pickled Harry or Chutney Mary. Indian society—Hindus, Muslims, and Sikhs—generally treated biracial men and women as outsiders. Some Anglo-Indians tried to pass as white and went to great lengths to keep their Indian blood a secret. In turn, British India had numerous cautionary tales about olive-skinned individuals trying to pass as Spanish or Portuguese. The stakes were high on both sides. Those who wished to pass knew that if their secret was revealed, they would face social ostracism or economic loss. Those who policed the racial lines feared that their culture would be endangered by alien invasion. Merle Oberon, a renowned Hollywood actress who appeared in such 1930s classics as *The Scarlet Pimpernel* and *The Dark Angel*, was Anglo-Indian, a fact she hid from the public until her death in 1979. Her nephew wrote a thinly disguised novel about her life, *Queenie*, which was later adapted into a mini-series for American television. Anglo-Indians in fiction, particularly women, are often portrayed as beautiful and a bit tragic. In this, the Anglo-Indian bears a faint resemblance to her distant literary cousin, the tragic mulatto of classic American fiction.

In time, Anglo-Indians developed their own culture, their own slang and cuisine. Due to the policies of the British Empire, many of them found jobs in the Indian Railways and Indian Telegraph Services. Some of them became schoolteachers in English-medium schools where they could teach children like me how to say Please and Thank You and Excuse Me and How Do You Do and Good Morning and Good Night prettily. Miss Solomon was quite a few shades darker than me, but her fluent English and her clothes made her more Westernized than I was. She taught me the English alphabet and introduced me to numbers. Most importantly, she gave me the ability to comprehend new information in a language that was still foreign to me. The first report card I received from her in 1975 has survived many decades and is still in my possession. I feel more sentimental about that old report card than I do about my Ivy League diplomas. In it, I can see a gentle teacher inviting a Bengali child into a new world of English. If I could see her today, I would surely rise from my chair and curtsy just as she taught me, and say, "Thank you, miss."

What Miss Solomon began would be carried forward

by a series of teachers—Hindu and Christian; Bengali, Punjabi, and Tamil. Very soon all of us girls were responding to our teachers in fluent English, gossiping among ourselves in English, and reading English books in our free time. I was formally introduced to reading and writing in English when I was four. At the age of five, I was formally introduced to reading and writing in my mother tongue, Bengali. I comprehended Hindi just as well as Bengali, but I would not learn how to read and write Hindi until I was nine. The Bengali girls spoke in Bengali to one another during recess, known as "tiffin time" back then, but we spoke in English to one another during class. The girls who came from other ethnolinguistic groups—Tamils, Biharis, Punjabis, Marathis, Marwaris—no doubt understood Bengali. Most of them had lived all their lives in Bengal. Yet, through some unspoken agreement, we spoke to one another only in English. It was to be our "link language"—the language that glued us girls from diverse linguistic groups together. Thomas Babington Macaulay would no doubt be very pleased at this turn of events.

We were all distant descendants of Lord Macaulay's "interpreter class"—a group of English-educated Indians prescribed by the British politician's infamous 1835 parliamentary speech, known as the "Minute on Indian Education." Many historians jokingly call it the longest minute in Indian history because one change in educational policy—the language in which some Indians were to be instructed—would bring about a seismic shift in Asia whose effects can be felt in global politics, business, and artistic production to this day.

Language joined us and divided us. Bengalis love stark binaries. We are born knowing there are two kinds of people in the world: Bengali and Non-Bengali. Black, white, Christian, pagan, Hindu, Muslim, straight, gay, rich, poor, skinny, fat, man, woman, friend, foe, Gryffindor, Slytherin—these categories vanish in the face of the main categorical divide in our world. Bengali and Non-Bengali. *Bangali. Abangali.* Once we separate out all the Non-Bengalis from the Bengalis, there is yet another division within the Bengali universe. Are you from *paschimbanga*, West Bengal, or from *purbabanga*, East Bengal? The question is of great importance to Bengalis and means absolutely nothing to other South Asians. West Bengalis are nicknamed *ghoti* and East Bengalis are nicknamed *bangal*. In the 1970s, we kept track of exactly what percentage of each category of blood ran through our veins, looking back at least two or three generations. When marriages were arranged, gossipy aunts asked leading questions in order to decipher if the bride's family was *ghoti* or if the groom's family was *bangal*. During soccer season in Calcutta, *ghoti*s supported the Mohun Bagan team and *bangal*s supported the East Bengal team. Three of my four grandparents counted places in *purbabanga*—Comilla, Khulna, Sylhet—as their ancestral homes. One grandparent counted Barrackpore in *paschim-*

banga as his ancestral home. That made me 75 percent *bangal* and 25 percent *ghoti*. During soccer season, I quietly rooted for the East Bengal team. When Mohun Bagan won, the fans celebrated victory with tiger prawns cooked in coconut milk. Hilsa fish cooked in a fiery mustard paste was the delicacy of choice for East Bengal victories. Small differences will always prove to be more divisive than the big ones, just as little traditions have more adhesive power than the great ones.

All the girls in my Catholic convent school—girls who repeated the Lord's Prayer four times a day, attended daily English elocution classes, learned Wordsworth poems by heart—knew who was Bengali and who was not, who was Hindu and who was not, who was *ghoti* and who was not. With the exception of one Sikh girl, the only non-Hindu girls were the Christian ones. The Christian girls kept themselves apart from us. In their case, it was not faith that divided us but social class. The religion once associated with the ruling Europeans was now largely the religion of converts from poorer segments of society in modern India. There were a few aristocratic Christian Indian families no doubt. In my school, however, the Christian girls were all "scholarship girls." A Christian charity paid for their tuition. They received free food during tiffin time. When we asked our Father in heaven to give us our daily bread, I did not understand that the Christian girls were receiving free loaves at school.

The Catholic nuns praised us for memorizing the Lord's Prayer and for reciting it with the correct English pronunciation. Among ourselves we knew that it was important to learn the prayer and the language, but stop short of conversion. We lived in a Hindu majority state in a Hindu majority nation. Being part of the dominant group meant being able to carelessly pick up some styles, words, affects of minority cultures, while maintaining our dominant status. A truly dominant group is unthreatened by minority cultures as long as they can be domesticated, consumed, transformed into an accessory, a condiment, a bit of swag.

I attended the convent school from the age of four until I was nearly twelve. This was where I learned algebra, geometry, biology, chemistry, physics, grammar, recitation, history, geography, literature, needlework, and art. Yet, I did not learn that my school was named after a Christian religious order founded on a mountain range in northern Israel in the twelfth century. I did not learn that the Book of Kings tells us there was an important altar to God on this very mountain. Pythagoras may have visited it. Tacitus wrote there was an oracle on the mountaintop. I did not know these stories.

· · ·

Each morning a gray school bus took me to the school and each afternoon the same bus dropped me home. We rented a one-bedroom flat on the ground floor of a three-story building. It was a typical south Calcutta house built around the middle of the twentieth century. The windows had wooden shutters and vertical iron bars. The bars were intended to provide security while still allowing us to buy small items from street hawkers throughout the day. The Kwality ice-cream man, the seller of savory flattened chickpeas, a neighbor who was returning a borrowed book—none of these people had to come inside our house to conclude their business. The iron bars were spaced just wide enough for us to pass a small ice-cream bar, a paperback, or even a little packet of snacks. If I wanted a balloon from the balloon man, or if Ma wanted to buy a new stainless steel cooking pot, the iron-barred windows would be our first point of contact. The final exchange would have to occur at our doorstep. Printed cotton curtains fluttered from each window, keeping the sun out. The walls in each room were painted a different pastel color and the floors were terrazzo. Tube lights lit up each room at night and ceiling fans cooled the rooms. The tube lights went dark and the fans came to a standstill when power shortages led to frequent brownouts. We called these power cuts "load shedding"—the electrical grid was overburdened and needed to shed its load. During load sheddings, everyone resorted to candles, kerosene lanterns, and hand fans made with palm leaves. Water shortages were common as well. Several plastic buckets filled with clean water always stood guard in one corner of our bathroom, in anticipation of that moment in the day when the taps would suddenly run dry.

Our home was located on Dover Lane—a residential street in the southern part of Calcutta. Our landlords were a middle-aged couple from Serampore, a small town near Calcutta. Once an important center of cotton and silk weaving, the area was colonized by the Danish in the eighteenth century, and subsequently came under British rule. Our landlords were part of a feudal family with a large estate in Serampore. The Dover Lane house was their city home. When I was a toddler, my parents had moved to this house from Asansol, a provincial town in West Bengal. Baba worked as a sales representative for an international pharmaceutical company in Calcutta. Ma looked after the running of the household. I was an only child, an increasingly common sight among educated, urban Indians looking to make a break from large households of the past.

All my memories begin in Dover Lane, Calcutta. I called our landlords Dadu and Didi—colloquial terms for grandfather and grandmother. Even though we were tenants, as the only child in the entire house, I was allowed to roam about every floor as I pleased. Dadu and Didi lived on the second and third floors, along with their two unmarried daughters and a maid. Their eldest daughter was married and lived outside Calcutta in a small coal-mining town where her husband was the colliery manager. The two younger daughters eventually married and left as well. Dadu,

Didi, and Sushila, the maid, lived upstairs and acted collectively as my proxy grandparents.

Our ground-floor residence was adjacent to the living quarters of the doorman, Hriday Singh. He lived alone in a single room that was creatively divided into three separate areas with plywood partitions. Darwanji, as I always called him, had come from a village in Uttar Pradesh, a state in northern India, and was a widower. His only child, a daughter, died young of a mysterious illness. He sent remittances back to his village every month. To make extra money he would wake up at four each morning and wash our neighbors' cars. Occasionally, he gave me a taste of the delicious food he cooked for himself on his kerosene stove. Okra stuffed with tangy spices and *dal puris*—crisp little fried flatbreads stuffed with asafetida-scented lentils—were his specialty. He took me for walks when my parents were too busy to go out in the evening. Our favorite destination was the clothing shops on Gariahat Road with mannequins displayed in the front. We would walk on the crowded sidewalks and he would point out all the mannequins draped in beautiful saris. For some reason unclear to me, he and I referred to the mannequins as "mummies." Some evenings, Darwanji would knock on our door and ask my parents if I wanted to go "see the mummies." If my parents assented, I would eagerly put on my sandals and walk out to bustling Gariahat Road, holding tightly on to Darwanji's hand.

Perhaps because he missed his own daughter, Darwanji

was always kind to the neighborhood kids. The little stoop outside his quarters was a popular hangout spot for children, maids, cooks, and drivers from all over the neighborhood. In a city where people rarely mixed outside of their social class, this stoop was a special spot. Hindi-speaking migrants who worked as drivers or cooks sat beside the Bengali-speaking children of their employers. We chatted in a mix of languages, watched neighbors go about their daily life, listened to the barking stray dogs, and enjoyed the Hindi film songs broadcast by All India Radio.

Sushila worked as a maid for Dadu and Didi upstairs. She was an elderly widow who had been in their service since the family's Serampore days. She put so much red chili paste in her fish curries that I would rarely eat the food upstairs. Ma and Baba employed a number of people as domestic help, and many of these people became an important part of my childhood. There was a live-in maid who usually helped with the cooking and attended to me. Another maid came in a couple of times a day to wash the dishes, do the laundry, and clean the floors. The *jamadar*, a man whose low caste condemned him to handling other people's waste, arrived each morning to clean the bathrooms and take away the household rubbish. The ironing was done by an *istriwallah* who set up shop in the neighborhood and ironed huge piles of starched cotton saris, shirts, and school uniforms. Without appliances such as washing machines, dishwashers, and vacuum cleaners, daily household tasks provided employment to a small army of people who moved in and out of our flat throughout the day.

Of the series of live-in maids who worked for us, Mundi and Jamuna were my favorites. These girls—no older than fifteen or sixteen, roughly the same age as my daughter as I write these words—came from villages in Bengal. Their fathers visited us once a month to collect their wages. I do not know if the girls received any portion of their wages. Mundi pierced my ears secretly one afternoon when I was five, at my own behest, and for her good deed was fired from her job by my parents. I can still recollect with perfect clarity Mundi's teenage hands confidently pushing an ordinary sewing needle through my earlobes. Wherever she is today, I wish I could tell her that each time I adorn my ears with jewelry, our stolen afternoon of girlish adventure shimmers into life for a brief spell. Jamuna told me wondrous stories about man-eating tigers that roamed the jungles outside the village from where she came. Minor deities from the Hindu pantheon played an outsize role in rural life and Jamuna brought all those gods and goddesses—the ones who protected villagers from diseases, who ensured a good harvest, who kept snakes and tigers away—to my Dover Lane home. She told me ghost stories and taught me folk dances from her village. Ma did not like these dances and promptly enrolled me in a local dance school where I began to be trained in the classical *bharatanatyam* style before Jamuna's low, rural movements could leave an indelible mark on my body.

Sometimes, when Ma was taking her afternoon nap, Jamuna and I still danced together in the small verandah behind the kitchen, our bare feet stomping on the ground, our hands on our swiveling hips.

Mundi's and Jamuna's villages were in the Sundarbans, a dense mangrove forest in the southernmost part of West Bengal. I had never been to the Sundarbans. In the Bengali imagination, the Sundarbans are as magical as the Forest of Arden in *As You Like It* or Prospero's island in *The Tempest*. It is a wild and primeval place, replete with danger and eroticism. Jamuna told me of life in this mangrove forest, where tigers roamed free and shrimp were so plentiful that one could merely scoop up a bit of pond water with a piece of muslin and come home with enough tiny crustaceans to make a delicious *lau chingri*—a Bengali dish of bottle gourd cooked with shrimp. In the big city, shrimp and prawns were expensive delicacies. I dreamed of living in Jamuna's village and feasting on *lau chingri* and rice every day.

Most of the residents of Dover Lane were middle or upper middle class. The majority of our neighbors were Bengali, with the exception of a Marwari family who lived right across the street from us. Marwari traders, originally from the northwestern state of Rajasthan, comprise an important community in Calcutta. Although we lived as neighbors, nodded to each other across our little street, politely attended each other's wedding feasts, we rarely socialized with them. An imaginary line divided the Marwaris from the Bengalis and each group coexisted without too many instances of intermarriage.

We had a few neighbors from the southern Indian states as well. We lumped them all into one category and derisively called them Madrasis. Whether they were actually from Madras—present-day Chennai—or not, they were all Madrasi to us North Indians. Now we must add yet another marker to our list of social divisions in India—North Indian and South Indian. A linguistic line divided the northern states from the southern ones. In the north, we spoke Indo-European languages such as Bengali, Hindi, Punjabi, Gujarati, and Marathi. In the south, they spoke Dravidian languages such as Tamil, Telugu, Malayalam, and Kannada. Each group had negative stereotypes of the other and saw themselves as possessing the superior language, the more refined culture, the better food.

I recall no Muslims in our neighborhood. I naively believed all Muslims lived in a neighborhood in Calcutta known as Park Circus. Occasionally, Baba would bring home *shemaiyer halua*, a rich dessert of vermicelli cooked in thickened milk and scented with cardamom, saffron, and rose water. It is often served around Eid al-Fitr when Muslims mark the end of Ramadan. Baba knew Muslims through work and some of them would send us special dishes to mark the holidays. My grandfather had Muslim graduate students whose doctoral theses he supervised. In neighboring Bangladesh millions of Bengali Muslims resided. I saw

Muslims in Hindi films—usually caricatured as men in fez-zes with kohl-lined eyes or tragic courtesans who sang of moths and flames—but I never played with Muslim girls in my neighborhood or sat next to one in school. Muslims were either poor minorities or legendary emperors of the past who built the Taj Mahal in Agra. We studied Mughal history in school. We knew that the Muslim *nawab* of Bengal, Siraj-ud-daula, had lost the battle of Plassey in 1757 to Robert Clive, ushering in British rule over India. Yet, those Muslims in the textbooks seemed to have no connection to the Muslims who lived in Park Circus and sent us *shemaiyer halua*.

The Bengali language is particularly rich in Persian, Arabic, and Turkish words. The common Bengali words for color, weather, temperament, fort, court, lawyer, client, crops, carpet, paper, pen, and inkwell were all brought to us by people who prayed facing Mecca. The list can go on. We do not normally think of these as loanwords. Just as you probably do not think of "algebra" or "horde" or "jungle" or "thug" as loanwords from Arabic or Turkish or Hindi when you are speaking in English. It is a wonderful thing that living languages can continually absorb new entrants and not impose visa restrictions on them. Bengali is no different from all other living languages in this aspect—its borders are open to immigration. It includes a treasure trove of words derived from Sanskrit, as well as from Persian, Arabic, and Turkish. Even China and Portugal gave us some words. Bengalis refer to an elected politician as *mantri*. Bengalis love to drink tea, or *cha*, multiple times a day. Both *mantri* and *cha* are words we have inherited from our neighbors to the north, the Chinese. Some mornings we Bengalis eat a slice of toasted *pao ruti* during our breakfast. The Portuguese brought us the word *pao*, but we rarely recall that at the breakfast table. Similarly, we do not always remember that our Persian brethren gave us words for color (*rang*) and weather (*aabohawa*). I did not grow up parsing words for their religion or place of origin. Unfortunately, I cannot say I treated people in the same way.

· · ·

We had another type of neighbor whose homes were all but invisible to kids of my social class. We knew of their existence, but we refused to even walk near their homes. Near our middle-class residential neighborhood was a slum. We called it the *basti*. The maids who came daily to clean our floor and fetch our drinking water from the tube well, the low-caste *jamadar* who cleaned our toilets and disposed of our rubbish, and the man who ironed our saris all lived in the *basti*. I never actually saw the slum. I had a vague notion of the area in which it was situated. There was a giant rubbish heap of construction waste and household trash at the end of one street. My friends always whispered that the *basti* was on the other side. I am not sure if this was correct, but the rubbish heap was a convenient boundary wall—one which no one really wanted to scale. Anything that lay on the other side of such a foul-smelling hill of rotting garbage was surely a dismal place.

Children the same age as me lived in that unseen slum—children of the *bastibashi*, the unlucky progeny of slum dwellers. I did not play with these children or even acknowledge their existence. I went to school, freshly bathed, liberally dusted with talcum powder, hair oiled and combed, in a starched and ironed uniform. I repeated the Lord's Prayer, curtsied to Sister Josephine, and learned to read and write in three languages and three scripts. The children of the *basti* were grimy, their bellies distended from malnutrition, their hair reddish brown from dust and sun, clothed in tattered garments, or perhaps not fully clothed at all. Some of the children had an amulet tied with a black thread around their waist or their arm. What more degradation was to be feared that a mother had tied an amulet to keep the evil eye away from her half-clothed child?

I remember the shade of paint on every wall of our flat. A pale peach living room. A seafoam green bedroom. I have no memory of the *basti*. I saw some slums in Hindi movies. And later, when I came to the United States, I saw more slums in Hollywood films about India. When I lived in India I was blind to them. The greatest division in a society is one that makes an entire group of humans simply invisible to us. When my friends and I chased cricket balls, soccer balls, and badminton shuttlecocks around our neighborhood we ran past these other children, just as we ran past the stray dogs and the rickshaws. We avoided them with the same practiced maneuvers as we did potholes in the streets or cow dung on the sidewalks. I wish I could tell you a different story. It would be much nicer to speak of myself as the noble protagonist of a feel-good American movie set in a colorful Third World country—the middle-class girl with a heart of gold who befriends the kid who sleeps on a sidewalk. I am not that noble character in a Third World story. I was neither the melodramatic villain who tortured the poor, nor an exemplary heroine who rescued them.

The daily violence we perpetuated on the children of the invisible slum was of a more insidious nature—all the more dangerous, for it was casual, perpetuated without premeditation, leaving no visible bloodstains or fingerprints on the crime scene. We pretended not to see those children. We pretended that they were not quite human like us. We kept our distance from them, never touching or speaking to them, lest their degradation infect our bodies like a deadly virus. Did the *bastibashi* and their children see us? Did they adjust their bodies so that we could run past them more quickly to catch a cricket ball or an errant shuttle-cock? Were they hungry when they saw us reaching through our barred windows to buy a Kwality ice cream in the afternoon? Did they experience rage when I walked out of our Dover Lane house each morning in my school uniform, my canvas rucksack bulging with books, my black Mary

Janes shining, the elastic edge of navy blue socks fitting
snugly against my calves? Did their knees hurt from squatting as they swabbed our terrazzo floors each day alongside
their mothers? Did they feel nauseous when they had to
clean our plates piled with oily fish bones and caked with
streaks of yellow lentils? These questions—questions each
human owes another—I can only ask from the safe distance of time. As a young girl, I did not ask them.

The children of the slum entered our homes only under
one circumstance. They came as their mother's assistant.
Some of the part-time maids brought their young children
along to help with the sweeping or washing. We always
knew the names of the children of our maids, even if we
rarely exchanged a word with them. It was customary to
address a maid using the name of her child. Prakasher Ma,
the Mother of Prakash, was one of our maids for a while.
Prakash was her young teenage son. Sometimes he accompanied her on the job. For reasons unknown to me, I liked
to watch him work. I remember a particular afternoon
when I watched him clean the bedroom. It is a movie scene
I can play endlessly in my mind. I am wearing a sleeveless
cotton frock and lying on the bed. I pretend to read a comic
book, but I am actually watching Prakash sweeping the
floor around me. I do not know why it is both thrilling and
soothing to watch him. Once he is finished sweeping, he
switches the ceiling fan back on and brings in a bucket of
water and a rag. Then he squats on the floor and starts

swabbing it in hypnotic semicircles. His skin is browner than mine, sunburnt and rough. The soles of his feet and the palms of his hands have a yellowish tinge. Prakash must be thirteen or fourteen. I am around ten. Etiquette demands that I leave the room when it is being cleaned. But I stay in the room. I know I am breaking a minor rule. Prakash knows this too. Every few seconds he lifts his head up and our eyes meet. I do not know what he is thinking. I sense he is angry. And I am not angry at all. I like watching him. After a while, Prakash stopped coming to work with his mother. I do not know if he ever attended school. I do not know what sort of job he found eventually. All I know is that for a while we were two Bengali children, a boy and a girl, in a room in Calcutta, less than two feet away from each other, who never exchanged a word because there existed no language to scale the wall that separated us.

The *basti*'s invisibility was an inverse function of its significance in our lives. Nowadays slum tourism is popular all over the world. People visit Dharavi in Bombay, favelas such as Rocinha in Rio de Janeiro, or townships in South Africa. Only those truly confident that they will not become slum dwellers themselves can go on such tours. I lack that confidence. The *basti* was a silent reminder of where I would end up if we slid downward. If I did poorly in school, if I married the wrong man, if my father lost his job, or if the Indian economy tilted in the wrong direction, we could end up on the other side of the garbage heap.

I could be swabbing the terrazzo floors daily while another child would lie on a bed with a book in her hand, watching me silently. The electric current that ran between Prakash and me was not simply a product of systematic inequality, of an unfair society that allowed me a fancy education and condemned him to illiteracy and a life of backbreaking labor. The electricity was also generated by a child's fearful sense of economic instability. Knowing that the color of a banana is yellow might have opened one set of doors for me, but the limbless beggars, the slum children, and the refugees who lived on railway platforms were daily reminders of the fragility of my comfortable life.

There was nothing antiseptic about my life in Calcutta. If I have recounted pleasant memories, do not imagine that I lived in a cocoon. As a child I read that when Prince Siddhartha was young, his father made sure that he never laid eyes on sickness, old age, or death. The Buddha became enlightened only after he gazed upon the sufferings of human life. I do not know what was required to keep all things unpleasant hidden from a prince in ancient Kapilavastu. My own eyes saw all manner of unpleasantness in the city of Calcutta. Corpses were carried to the cremation ground on biers through the main thoroughfares. *Bolo hari, hari bol.* That was the traditional chant of Hindus taking the dead to be cremated. Married women had their feet reddened with *alta*, a cosmetic dye traditionally formulated with lac, after death. Seeing the red feet on a bier always made me nauseous, even though I knew that it was a wife's great fortune to die before her husband. Widows were doomed to a life without pleasure, and allowed no color other than white. Yet, those red feet of corpses gave me the chills. When my father's Lambretta scooter took us past a particular open-air crematorium in south Calcutta, I always held my breath.

I saw children with wounds, missing limbs, blind eyes, and stunted growth begging in traffic stops for a few coins. I was always told that if I let go of my parents' hands in a crowd, I would be kidnapped, maimed, and turned into one of those beggar children. The kidnappers were called *chheledhora* and they were the bogeyman of Calcutta. Hindi films of that era often used these kidnappers as a plot device—in a crowded fair, a child is separated from his parents and is forced into a life of crime. The lucky sibling who did not let go of his mother's hand grows up at home and becomes a respectable citizen. In some of the Hindi movies of that era, lost children were raised by members of other communities. A Hindu boy might be raised as a Muslim or a Christian, be given a new name, a new destiny. Ma dug her nails into my wrist when she led me through Calcutta streets, fearful of losing me in the crowd that pushed up against us from all sides.

I saw dogs run over by buses. I saw cows, crows, and naked children eating scraps found in the same garbage heap. I saw the ropey, sweaty muscles of rickshaw pullers straining to carry me and my family from one neighborhood to another. Calcutta was one of the last big cities in India to allow hand-pulled rickshaws to operate when most other cities had moved on to cycle rickshaws. I saw these rickshaw pullers hunched over their noontime meal on the sidewalk. There was a rickshaw puller "restaurant" near our home. Every afternoon half a dozen men ate *chhatu* on dented aluminum plates on the sidewalk. Their skin was dark brown from constant exposure to the sun. Dressed only in a *lungi*, a simple piece of cloth wrapped around the waist like a sarong, their bodies were thin and bent with hard labor coupled with too few calories. The rickshaw puller's noonday meal consisted of a portion of chickpea flour that a roadside vendor sold them. The humble *chhatu*—sometimes called *sattu* in other parts of India—was formed into a soft dough with some water and salt. To add a bit of taste, sometimes the men ate it with a green chili and a chunk of raw onion. After they finished, they washed their own plates and lay down for a bit of rest in the shade of their rickshaws. If a paying customer suddenly materialized, the rickshaw puller would be off again, tugging people like us through traffic snarls and unrelenting heat.

I saw all of this. I saw the bodies that labored to keep me in comfort. I saw the animals we ate. In fact, as a treat, I was allowed to choose the hen that we would eat for lunch. In Gariahat market, my mother would ask me to choose the bird from the coop. I always chose the prettiest one. A boy would grab the fluttering bird, take it to the back—*whack whack whack*—and he would hand us a still-warm parcel wrapped in newspaper a few minutes later. Freshly slaughtered goat carcasses swung from hooks, waiting for the butcher's block. Live fish were killed, scaled, skinned, and chopped. And all this would go into our plastic market basket, along with fresh vegetables, fruits, and other provisions. The turmeric, cumin, and coriander were always freshly ground. The garlic-ginger-onion-chili paste was prepared daily. Occasionally, a coconut was chopped open and its milky, white flesh was scraped using a special metal instrument reserved only for coconuts. Our kitchen emanated all sorts of aromas—spicy, herbal, vegetal, animal, fishy. And it also smelled of sweat. The sweat of the maid who ground the spices. The sweat of the maid's boy who cleaned up after her. The sweat of a girl who watched all this calmly and carried within her a small lump of terror—one slip and her world could be rearranged. Ours was a society built precariously on deep inequalities. These inequalities extracted sweat from all our glands, the winners and losers, the bourgeoisie and the slum dweller, the *bhadralok* and the *bastibashi*.

The bent body that pulls the rickshaw and the well-groomed one that sits atop it. The callused hands that grind the spices and the soft fingers that delicately mix a fragrant fish curry with rice at the lunch table. The one who extends a malnourished hand to beg for a coin or a piece of bread and the one who is carried off to Chinese restaurants on Park Street to feast on Hakka noodles and tutti-frutti ice cream. The refugee who lives and dies on a railway platform and the girl who sits at Flury's cake shop enjoying a petit four with her father as a reward for doing well on an exam. The line between these two groups is fragile and requires precise maintenance at all times. Young Siddhartha may have been shielded from all scenes of suffering, but I was not. Yet, I never took full measure of my own privileges until one day, in another country, I became the one who looked on enviously as others rushed past me to seize a dazzling prize, immersed in the sweat-soaked thrill of their own game, barely taking notice of my presence.

•   •   •

I had never seen a sandy beach or snow before I left India. I had traveled to the foothills of the Himalayas only once with Ma and Baba on a family trip to Mussoorie, a hill station in northern India. Ma and Baba had never left India before we came to the United States. None of my four grandparents had left India. Two of my grandparents were born in a part of Bengal that is no longer in India. Their birthplaces were part of Pakistan from 1947 to 1971 and are currently part of Bangladesh. We did not count such accidents of geopolitics as "having been abroad." One of my great-grandfathers was born in England to Indian parents and arrived in India later in life. He never left India after he settled down and married an Indian woman. My foreign-born great-grandfather, George Banerji, makes a single cameo appearance within a minor chapter of British Indian legal history—the 1916 case of *George Banerji vs. Emperor*. My great-grandfather was discovered using a bicycle with a motor-wheel attachment without a license. I can only imagine the story of a young Indian barrister, born in London and newly arrived in India, who had to appear before a British judge at the Allahabad High Court for the seemingly comical crime of riding an unlicensed motorized bicycle. By the time I was born, my great-grandfather had passed away, the British colonizers had departed, and the streets of independent India were congested with millions of motorized two-wheelers.

One of my cousins lived in Japan during the 1970s. Her visits were highly anticipated by our family. She seemed very glamorous to me. She traveled regularly on an airplane, spoke Japanese, and had tasted exotic foods. My cousin brought me two pairs of white socks from Japan during one of her visits to Calcutta. One was a pair of white ankle socks with a lace edge. I wore this pair on the plane when I first came to America. The other was a pair of kneesocks with two cherries on them. Both pairs were made of nylon. I wore the cherry socks to school once, defying our strict uniform rules. I was proud of those cherries decorating my calves. I thrilled at the tightness of that elastic band cutting into my legs. In my imagination those Japanese socks gave me a tenuous connection to the sophisticated world beyond India. My cousin who lived in Japan also gave me a plastic pencil box with an American football player on it. The box's magnetic closure was especially satisfying. I loved to open and close the box repeatedly, and listen to the metallic sound of the magnet clicking the lid into place. The Japanese pencil box was too special to take to school regularly. On exam days, I took it to school as a good-luck charm.

Baba's older brother had immigrated to Texas when I was still a baby. When his family visited us occasionally, we caught glimpses of the United States. My aunt's makeup, the fabric of my cousin's pants, the small gifts they brought us—they were signs of prosperity and modernity. One year my uncle gave us a bouquet of white plastic daisies and a buttery yellow breakfast set made of "unbreakable" melamine. The flowers were displayed permanently in a brass vase on top of our fridge. No visitor to our home could miss the daisies that never wilted in the Calcutta heat. The yellow breakfast set was never opened. It seemed like a sacrilege to do so. I knew of no one who owned a set of dishes just for eating breakfast. The United States seemed like a fairy-tale place where breakfast required its own special set of unbreakable cups and plates.

Once a cousin flew to Britain to visit a relative. She brought me back a wide-tooth plastic comb and small plastic doll. It was not a Barbie, but I did not know that at the time.

It was the only doll I had with dainty pointed feet always ready for tiny high-heel pumps. I was fascinated by the smell of that plastic doll—a whiff of vanilla and something faintly medicinal. The smell often tempted me to take a nibble on the plastic limbs. I imagined England smelled like that. Ma's brother went to Nepal on his honeymoon—it was quite a daring and stylish thing to do in the mid-1970s—and he brought me back a red nylon T-shirt. Suddenly my cotton frocks, blouses, and skirts seemed very frumpy next to the nylon T-shirt.

All these materials—the nylon, the plastic, the melamine—were associated with upward mobility and the West during the 1970s. Our own Indian cottons and silks were suddenly passé. Indian women started wearing nylon saris. Indian men sported nylon shirts and polyester pants. In the early decades of the twentieth century, Gandhi had urged Indians to boycott foreign goods as part of our struggle against British rule. The spinning wheel and handloom cotton were the symbols of freedom from Western imperialism. Our grandparents wore cottons, silks, and wools. The cloth was woven in India. The garments were stitched by local tailors, *darzi*s. But now it was fashionable to wear factory-made synthetic clothes, imported jeans and T-shirts. Baba had a pair of navy blue polyester pants. My mother acquired a few nylon saris. To wear polyester bell-bottoms, ride a Lambretta scooter, eat in Park Street restaurants, and watch the latest Hindi film in an air-conditioned cinema hall was my idea of living the Westernized good life in Calcutta during the 1970s.

• • •

Cinema was the great window to the world beyond Calcutta. Metro, Globe, Roxy, Lighthouse, New Empire, Priya, Menaka. The names of these cinema halls promised three air-conditioned hours of thrills, comedy, tragedy, and most importantly, travel. Hindi movies nearly always included song sequences that transported us to lakes in Kashmir, deserts in Rajasthan, beaches in Goa, tulip fields in Holland, or snowy slopes in Switzerland. James Bond films—a favorite of my parents—were a world tour in themselves. And Bruce Lee had already taken me to Hong Kong.

As a child I needed an adult to take me to the cinema hall. But I could roam all over the world unchaperoned when I had a book in my hand. *Phantom* and *Archie* comics, *Nancy Drew*, *Hardy Boys*, and Agatha Christie kept me company during the evenings when load shedding darkened Dover Lane. I read by candlelight even though my parents said it would ruin my eyes. I devoured everything the controversial British children's author Enid Blyton ever wrote, and had no idea of her shabby reputation in her native country. I read Bengali books with great gusto as well. *Raj Kahini* (Royal Tales) by Abanindranath Tagore, brother of Rabindranath, took us children on a quasi-historical journey through Rajasthan. *Aam Antir Bhepu* by Bibhutibhushan Bandyopadhyay (translated into the Apu Trilogy films by Satyajit Ray) made us weep. We sat beside the young Apu in a train carriage, as he sped away from his ancestral village. His dead sister, Durga, pleaded with us not to be left behind. *Chander Pahar* (Mountain of the Moon), written by the same author who gave us Apu's tale, took us to Uganda in search of diamonds.

Bengali children had their own homegrown Sherlock Holmes in the detective stories of Byomkesh, Feluda, and Professor Shonku. We collected *Amar Chitra Katha* comics, modeled loosely on the *Classics Illustrated* series published in the United States between the 1940s and the 1970s. Hergé's *Tintin* comics were very popular—in both English and Bengali—but high prices kept them out of the reach of children whose families lived under straitened circumstances. The lucky boy or girl who had a few *Tintin*s lying around at home was cajoled regularly by other children to share those coveted comics. You should hear Captain Haddock swear, Bianca Castafiore sing, and Snowy bark in Bengali. We knew that English cows *moo* and English dogs *woof* and English guns go *bang bang*. We also knew that Bengali cows say *hamba* and Bengali dogs say *bhou bhou* and Bengali guns go *gurum gurum*.

While television was still a rarity in middle-class homes in the 1970s, radio was ubiquitous. On Sundays, we listened to popular radio dramas and quizzes sponsored by

Bournvita, a brand of chocolate malt drink manufactured by Cadbury. The news, in Bengali and English, and Hindi film music programs were the background score to our daily lives. During test match season, cricket commentary on the radio could be heard in every home and at every corner shop. My grandparents owned a large radio that was lovingly covered by an embroidered cloth when not in use. My parents owned a smaller radio. As a child, I spent hours staring at it while listening to various programs, imagining miniature beings talking and singing inside the machine. The visual feast of the large Hindi movie screen whisked me off to colorful Dutch tulip fields where lovers ran toward each other in slow motion; the tiny beings who existed within our transistor radio showed me other realms, and other lives, solely through the magic of sound.

Between 1975 and 1977, India was besieged by the Emergency, a period of twenty-one months when Prime Minister Indira Gandhi canceled elections and suspended many civil liberties. During the 1970s, when the very freedom our grandparents and parents had realized at great cost during the 1940s hung in the balance, children's books transported us to the Aravalli Hills in Rajasthan, to the Richtersveld in South Africa, to Archie, Betty, and Veronica's Riverdale High School in America, to the English boarding schools of Cornwall where Enid Blyton sent her fictional characters, and to Harun al-Rashid's Baghdad of the *Arabian Nights*. The detective fiction, adventure stories, boarding school novels, science fiction, and comic books—in both Bengali and English—sharpened the blurry edges of Dover Lane. Reading a boys' adventure story set in Uganda made me scramble for our well-worn family atlas. When I looked up Uganda, my finger traced the distance between my own city and Africa across the gutter of the book. When I read about the romantic Rajasthani past, I understood that India stretched far beyond the borders of Bengal. When I laughed along with Archie, Reggie, and Jughead, I had a vague notion of American life and began to measure my own distance from it. A promiscuous reader, I was a true fan of Enid Blyton stories, *Tintin* comics, and *Nancy Drew* and *Hardy Boys* mysteries. I also sensed—with a child's clumsy shrewdness—that the characters on the page belonged to the West and I did not.

Since childhood, we knew that books were sacred and paper was precious. Books were rarely thrown away. They belonged to the realm of Saraswati, the goddess of knowledge and music. In the early spring, when Saraswati *puja*—the special day for worshipping the goddess—appeared on the Hindu calendar, young children and students were unmatched in their devotion. All of us, wearing yellow-hued outfits, would lay our books at the goddess's feet and repeat the mantra chanted by the priest. To this day, the only Sanskrit mantra I know is the one we offer to Saraswati, the divine one who carries a *pustak*, a book, in her hand. Orange and yellow marigolds are the traditional floral offerings for Saraswati. We would collect the flowers, blessed by the goddess, and press them between the pages of our books. If one was falling behind in a particular subject at school, the relevant textbook would be liberally stuffed with marigold petals. Years later, pressed, pale orange marigold petals occasionally flutter out of my few remaining childhood books.

I never let those marigold petals fall to the ground if I can help it. I rush to catch them midflight before they are defiled by my feet. The goddess of knowledge has a vast domain. Her flowers are enchanted. As are all books and all printed paper. I can never let a book touch my feet or fall on the ground. If such an inauspicious accident happened, I would immediately press the book to my lips and forehead. The written word cannot be disrespected, for it might anger the goddess of knowledge. Since infancy I had been taught that we could not risk Saraswati's departure from our lives.

Paper was valued for another reason. It had monetary value. We did not recycle because we were environmentally conscious. We recycled because it had direct economic benefits. The Bengali version of rag-and-bone men were regular visitors to middle-class homes—looking to buy old glass bottles, newspapers, books, writing pads, and torn saris. We watched money exchange hands every month when old newspaper stacks, notebooks that could no longer be reused, and empty glass bottles were taken away by these

rag-and-bone men. Simply putting these items in a recy-
cling bin would have been unthinkable. Besides, the city
provided us no such bins in those days.

During the 1970s, the information highway that con-
nected me to other worlds—European, African, American,
and Asian—was made of sacred and valuable paper.

· · ·

India has a much longer recorded history than the United
States. Yet, the Indian city from which I departed was in
fact a little bit younger than the American city where I
settled. In the late 1600s, three villages situated at the
mouth of the Hooghly River in eastern India—Kalikata,
Gobindapur, and Sutanuti—began the journey toward ur-
banization that would result in the city of Calcutta. It has
been renamed Kolkata in recent times in order to shed its
colonial orthography. For Bengalis of my age, it is hard to
stop calling it Calcutta when we speak in English.

The city where I arrived as an immigrant, Cambridge,
is located north of Boston, across the Charles River. Cambridge and Calcutta are both cities that were founded in the
1600s. Cambridge is approximately sixty years older than
Calcutta. That makes it one of the oldest cities in the United
States. Calcutta, on the other hand, is one of the relatively
new Indian cities, far younger than Delhi, for instance.
Both cities were once part of the British Empire. One could
say I was simply traversing the old routes left behind by a

dead empire when I arrived in Cambridge from Calcutta as a twelve-year-old.

Air travel leads us to see the world as a place of absolute differences. As a girl, I boarded a plane in Calcutta and landed in Doha, the capital of Qatar. The plane that took off from Qatar dropped us off in London. A final flight took us across the Atlantic. India. Qatar. Britain. The United States. These are nations with clear boundaries, distinct from each other. One would be forgiven for thinking that human beings change abruptly when we cross an imaginary line on the ground, the line we call national borders. Languages, religions, tastes, beliefs, hair color, skin color, and even the shapes of bodies change when we cross borders. Except they do not.

Before flying on a plane, I traveled many miles on trains. Each year we visited my maternal grandparents in Allahabad, a town in northern India. We took the Bombay Mail from Calcutta in the late evening and reached Allahabad around lunchtime the next day. It was one of my favorite journeys. My mother packed us a special dinner of *luchi* and *alur dom*. Little disks of fried flatbread and potatoes cooked in a tangy yogurt sauce. We ate dinner after we passed Bardhaman station. Then I climbed onto the top bunk of our three-tier carriage and prepared to fall asleep listening to the chatter of our fellow passengers and the rhythmic thumping of the carriage as we sped westward. The train stopped at Gaya, a city in Bihar, usually after

I had fallen asleep. Occasionally, drowsy with sleep, I heard the voices of people getting on board at Gaya. Bengali slowly gave way to Hindi with a distinct Bihari accent. The next morning, I awoke as the train pulled into Mughalsarai junction. It meant we had crossed from Bihar into Uttar Pradesh. This was when my parents drank their morning tea. Small clay cups of milky tea were purchased through the train's window. *Chai garam! Garam chai!* The tea seller's voice was the sweetest of alarm clocks. Now I knew we were getting closer to our destination, where my grandparents, uncles, and cousins waited. The Hindi of eastern Uttar Pradesh slowly filled my world, as I climbed down from the upper bunk and started watching the fields and small towns roll by. The station names were written in different scripts. The familiar coconut trees and toddy palms of Bengal gave way to other trees. I could tell which state we were in by detecting the exact shade of green outside the train, by noting the way in which a woman wore her sari as she walked along a mud path, and even by watching cattle grazing on fields as our train sped toward Allahabad.

I knew we Indians from different states were unlike one another. I saw this on the train journey every year. I also knew that changes did not occur abruptly. There was no sudden difference in language, dress, or food when the Bombay Mail rolled across a state line. The slow accretion of minute changes—the subtlest of variations in how we pronounced a word, or shaped a letter, or spiced the *samosa*s—added up over a day until I could truly see the diversity of the subcontinent in its fullest bloom.

The Bombay Mail connects Calcutta on the eastern coast of India to Bombay on its western coast. It was the ethnographic laboratory of my childhood. I relished our national diversity and internalized our hierarchies. I could not, however, imagine that there were yet other differences and hierarchies in the larger world beyond India and one day they would transform the girl who loved sleeping on the upper bunk of a three-tier Indian Railways train.

Chapter Two

. . .

The First Remove

The first morning I woke up in America I could smell bacon frying. I was nearly twelve years old. I had spent the night sleeping in the living room of Baba's childhood friend. This friend, an architect and the grandson of one of modern India's most influential artists, was married to a white woman. She was cooking us breakfast in the adjoining kitchen when I opened my eyes. Their duplex apartment was right across the Charles River from Harvard Square. My parents slept in one of the two bedrooms on the top level, while our host and his wife had the other bedroom. The couch was allotted to me. It was a modest apartment. As a parochial Bengali girl, I had envisioned the wealthy West as the land of opulent overstuffed sofas, velvet drapes, crystal vases, and expensive carpets. This home was utterly confusing to my eyes. The dining chairs were made of metal tubes and woven cane; the lamps looked like crushed white paper balloons. I had imagined America was the land of rich people with air-conditioning, big cars, cities laid on grids, and skyscrapers. A new world, a young country where everything sparkled and smelled good, unlike Indian cities where ruins, rick-shaws, crooked gullies, and the smell of oldness prevailed.

When I opened my eyes that morning, the first thing I saw was a triangular neon CITGO sign. I had no way of knowing that this had been a beloved Boston icon since 1940. Being an immigrant child before the era of the Inter-net, Wikipedia, or Google, I was seeing America for the first time.

It was a week of many firsts for me. I had flown on a plane. I had traveled outside India. I had bacon for break-fast. Even now, if I get too complacent about my sense of belonging here—my ability to speak, dress, look, think like an American—I only need to smell bacon frying and I am a newly arrived immigrant again. That morning, I smelled it, heard it sizzling and crackling, before I tasted it. It was a complex animal smell, making my mouth water and my stomach churn in revulsion at the same time. Today, my favorite sandwich is a BLT. I greedily search for those salty bits of bacon in a Cobb salad. Yet, the actual smell of bacon frying is a powerful reminder that I did not always relish these tastes, that there was a time when I struggled to train my palate according to the custom of this country.

Immigrants are supposed to be delighted when they arrive in America—huddled masses who have reached their final destination. But in 1982, I was sad when our British Airways plane landed at Boston's Logan Airport. Baba, who originally trained as a geologist, and spent most of his working life in India as a sales representative for pharmaceutical companies, had been unemployed for many years. Since the late '70s, our middle-class life in Dover Lane had been sliding imperceptibly toward the unseen *basti* behind the garbage dump. My *bharatanatyam* classes ended because the fees for the dance school had become a luxury we could no longer afford. The number of maids we employed dwindled as the household budget shrunk. Fish and fowl appeared fewer times on the menu until one day they disappeared completely. Ma went less frequently to the tailor to order new dresses for me. Instead, we waited for the autumn, when my aunts sent us the customary gift of new fabric—a few meters of printed cotton, enough to make a dress for a young girl—for Durga *puja*. We began avoiding family weddings because we could not buy appropriate presents for the new couple. We stopped going to the nicer cinema halls of Calcutta and began to patronize the shabbier ones where ticket prices were lower. Those trips to Park Street restaurants such as Waldorf or Sky Room became a distant memory. We went there only when a better-off friend or relative treated us to a night out. The blue Lambretta was brought indoors and stowed away in our hallway as a reminder of happier times when we could afford the price of petrol. The sofa and coffee table vanished one day and instead of buying new furniture, we began renting it. Because new school uniforms were expensive, the hems of my blue school skirts had been taken down one too many times. I used to rub my finger over the light blue line, the part of the fabric that had been bleached with repeated washes and ironings. Each time the hem was taken down, the faded line of the old edge became a token of my precarious status as a member of the bourgeoisie. I began to ask girls who were older than me if I could buy their old school textbooks because new textbooks were beyond our budget.

As it happened, our downward mobility coincided with a meteoric rise in my grades at school. The more we moved toward the unseen world where Prakash and his mother lived, the better I performed in my examinations. In our brutal Indian school system of ranking students, I used to be ranked among the bottom five girls in a class of forty. That was when I was six or seven years old. Baba became unemployed when I was nine. Suddenly I was appearing in the top ten, then top three, and by the time I was eleven, I was consistently ranked first in my class after our examination marks were announced. Yet, I had to ask around school for a set of used textbooks as each new school year approached. I was no longer able to invite all my classmates for my birthday party where a cake from Flury's, decorated with marzipan roses, would have pride of place at the table. No matter how hard my mother tried to keep my uniforms clean and ironed, my blouses were never as white as those of the girls whose parents bought them new uniforms each year.

I became friends with the school bus driver's daughter, who was enrolled as a scholarship kid. She was one of the girls who received a free loaf of bread during tiffin time. I never ate bread that tasted so delicious, when she began sharing them with me during the bus ride home. Other girls might go home to daintier snacks. I saw such homes in advertisements. Tidy middle-class Indian homes riding the wave of upward mobility. Homes with televisions that children watched with their parents; with refrigerators filled with rows of soft drink bottles; with toaster ovens in which beaming mothers baked cakes for their kids who returned from school looking as dewy-fresh as they had left in the morning. But children in downwardly mobile homes know that an atmosphere of fear, resentment, anger, and dejection awaits them at home. One wrong move, and the whole house can explode. One mention of extra money needed for a field trip, or the cost of a new dress for the school chorus, or an art assignment that requires costly materials, and everything can go up in flames. As much as I hated the crowded, hot school bus, I was in no rush to return to Dover Lane. The bus driver's daughter and I enjoyed the free bread at the back of the bus, and she tantalized me with promises of fluffy kittens. My new friend seemed to have an endless access to kittens and each afternoon she promised that she would sneak one into school for me. She strung me along in this manner for months, describing the kittens in great detail.

I tried, with partial success, to mask the bitter taste of genteel poverty with the sweet taste of arrogance. Arrogant—there is no other word for how I felt when I sat on those rented chairs in our drawing room and studied my report card at the end of each term. A row of beautiful numbers—95, 96, 97, 98—written neatly in blue fountain pen ink. Those numbers made me feel strong when, in reality, I was weak and vulnerable. A girl in a poor Indian home during the 1970s had limited options, even if she possessed an English-medium education and her grand-father's name elicited looks of admiration and her great-grandfather once sailed from England wearing beautifully tailored suits. If I were to maintain the crucial space between myself and the boy who swabbed the floor, and Dar-wanji who washed cars at four a.m., and Jamuna whose father collected her monthly wages, and the maimed children who begged on the streets, I needed more than faded photographs of my ancestors leaning against elegant teak furniture.

In an irrational act of generosity, the Architect arranged a job for Baba as a salesman in a men's clothing store in Cambridge, Massachusetts. He helped us apply for green cards—a process that took nearly three years, over a quarter of my life at that point. The Architect had immigrated to the United States in the 1960s and studied design at Harvard. He had lost touch with Baba for many years until one day he decided to look us up in Calcutta. Spontaneously, he decided to help his unemployed friend and his family. Immigration routes are patterned on kinship networks. Brothers follow brothers. Children follow parents. Grandparents follow grandchildren. Through marriage these networks become ever more expansive and intricate. A new bride follows a husband. A few years later her mother might follow. Then her brother and his wife. Entire districts from certain parts of the world might find themselves in a small American town as families follow one another across well-established migratory paths. A new immigrant feels secure knowing there is a brother with whom one could stay for a few months until a job is arranged. A cousin might provide just the right tip to secure employment in a new country.

Occasionally, friendship trumps kinship. A sibling might distance himself from his less successful brother, and kinfolk might slowly inch away from a family member emitting the faint whiff of poverty. In a poor society, impecunity is treated as a communicable disease. If you stand too close to poverty, you might catch it. Others see the poor as lacking merit and virtue. We were becoming infectious, virtueless, without merit. And suddenly, just as I had begun to adjust to a slightly lower social class by giving up the little luxuries—new school uniforms, meat at the table, the use of a scooter—a long-lost friend led us to a new life. Without accruing any financial benefits for himself, without any social or moral obligations, what was the Architect's motivation? Perhaps he remembered rainy afternoons spent chatting over hot tea in a canteen. Maybe he recalled the red laterite soil of his hometown. He could have missed speaking Bengali with someone who knew him as a boy. Or maybe he wanted to be near someone who knew how to pronounce his name correctly. Perhaps he wanted to fashion three new immigrants into his ideal of the American nuclear family. I can only guess. The Architect might have been reaching for his past in his own irrational way. He might have wanted a second chance at rectifying mistakes he made as a foreign student in the America of the 1960s. I became the unintended beneficiary of his whimsy.

We waited for almost three years in India for our visas because Baba was too nervous to emigrate without a green card. We were making a historic leap from one continent to another, yet we were an extremely risk-averse family. Many immigrants carry these twin traits within themselves and some even pass them on to the next generation. As risk takers we leap far from the safety of home. Having left the comforts of home we know all too well that there is no safety net of kinship or citizenship to catch us should we topple. This makes us cautious. We check the lock on the door three times before going out. We save more than we spend. We collect sugar and ketchup packets from McDonald's and cannot throw anything away. At work, we beat every deadline in the office and never pass up a second gig to make extra money. We tell our children to keep their heads down, study hard, and always look for a bargain. As risk-averse immigrants, we do not rock the boat. If you were a trapeze artist without a net below you, wouldn't you act the same way? Anything else would be irrational.

Scholars who study immigrants such as Baba and Ma would describe them as the classic example of *Homo economicus*. Economic man makes rational decisions that will increase his wealth and his ability to buy nice things. In those early days in America, whenever people asked why my parents immigrated I felt a sense of irritation and embarrassment. I could not say that we were fleeing war or political turmoil. We were not exiles seeking political or religious freedom. We were seeking economic gains. We were seeking more money. That is a humiliating thing for a twelve-year-old girl to have to repeat in a schoolyard. My parents sounded greedy. Or, worse, they sounded like people who had failed to be successful in the country of their birth and sought a second chance in a richer country. Because I arrived with them, I feared I too was tainted by these labels—greedy, unsuccessful, *Homo economicus*. At twelve I had made no rational choice, but the accident of my birth made me *Homo economicus* all the same.

I wished we could pretend to be expats. Expats are

glamorous and cosmopolitan. Cool expats like Ernest Hemingway sip Bellinis in Harry's Bar in Venice. Modern expats are the well-heeled white Europeans or Americans one encounters in cities such as Dubai, Singapore, and Shanghai. They are foreigners who have moved to distant shores for all the same reasons as a humble immigrant— higher wages, more job opportunities, greater purchasing power, and faster upward mobility. White expats often hold themselves apart from natives in the Middle East, Africa, or Asia, seeing themselves as superior. They send their children to the local American, British, French, or German school. They go to restaurants and shops frequented by others who share their tastes. They have their own clubs. In the West, we do not begrudge white expats their seclusion. New immigrants in America, by contrast, are perceived as undesirables who bring down the real estate value of a neighborhood. The women wear strange garb, their ill-mannered children run amok, and their grocery stores emit unpleasant odors. Meanwhile, white expats add value to their surroundings. Shanghai's French Concession is chic because of the presence of white folk. European expats add glamour to the high-end restaurants of Abu Dhabi.

We weren't chic expats or political dissidents with lofty ideologies. We were three people moving from a country with fewer resources to one with greater resources. I doubt we added glamour or value to our surroundings.

"Why did your parents come to America?"

"For better jobs."

To this day this small exchange—repeated endlessly throughout my years in the United States—instantly determines the social hierarchy between my interlocutor and me. I wish I could say my parents possessed some extraordinary professional skill for which an American institution wooed them. We did not hold noble political or religious convictions that were at odds with the government of India. There was no war raging in my city and we were not being resettled. *Homo economicus* has a duller, more prosaic story to tell.

"Why did your parents come to America?"

"For better jobs."

The native-borns nod and feel pleased that they are citizens of a country that offers better everything—jobs, homes, clothes, food, schools, music. I would feel the same if I was in their shoes. It must feel good to be born in a country that has more wealth than other places, to have the hardest currency in your wallet. It must feel good to be generous and invite others—after intense vetting and preselection—to share in this plenty. Even though I had no say at all in my family's decision to emigrate, I felt my shoulders weighed down with the plenitude of the host country. This plenitude of which I was to be the grateful recipient was evidence that white people were superior to people like me. How else could one nation be so wealthy and another be so poor; one country have so much to give and another stand in a queue to receive? The inequality of nations was surely a sign that some races were morally, physically, and intellectually superior to others. The inequality of nations surely had nothing to do with man, but was shaped by Providence.

"Why did your parents come to America?"

"For better jobs."

• • •

Poor people anywhere in the world are very conscious of their clothes and personal appearance. When you venture out for an important occasion you wear your cleanest clothes, your least shabby footwear, with your body washed and your hair neat. If you have only one set of good clothes, you make sure it is washed and ironed even though you have to be naked when washing and ironing those precious articles of clothing. Shabby chic and bohemian disarray are for the rich. We were determined to arrive in the United States looking as sartorially polished as possible. Distinguishing ourselves from those slum dwellers, the ones who lived in the *basti*, was crucial. I had practiced eating with a fork in my left hand and a knife in my right hand for a week. I was determined not to be bested by the European food served during the flight. I practiced my conversational English. We planned our outfits days in advance.

Baba in his best suit, Ma in a red-and-cream silk sari

printed with a floral motif, and me in a dark gray, pleated wool skirt, yellow blouse, black Mary Janes, and white Japanese ankle socks—we had dressed for a special event. We left India with five suitcases, a mossy green carry-on bag made of fake leather, and sixty U.S. dollars. In retrospect, I realize we had less than sixty dollars. My parents were in debt to the Architect, who had loaned us the money for the airfare from Calcutta to Boston. Two Calcutta taxis, modeled after the old British Morris Minor, took us and our relatives to the airport. My maternal uncles and grandmother had come to Calcutta from Allahabad—an overnight train journey—to bid us farewell. Back then, there was a gallery at Calcutta's Dum Dum Airport from where one could wave to passengers as they boarded the plane on the tarmac. One of my uncles had brought a small flashlight with him and had told Ma that he would wave it. Even if we were too far away in our plane to make out the faces of our relatives, we would know from that flashing point of light that they were there. They would not leave until our plane departed Indian soil. It was dark when our flight took off. I saw the flashlight bobbing up and down in the distance.

Our plane stopped in Doha, Qatar, for refueling, but the passengers were not allowed to disembark. Then came a long layover at Heathrow. With the small amount of money that we had, my parents had to be careful with their purchases. They bought a little tube of moisturizer (for none of us knew how dehydrating planes could be) and a medium-sized bar of white chocolate. I was familiar with Cadbury chocolates in India. But white chocolate was a revelation. We carefully broke it into three equal pieces and savored the taste. And then we boarded another plane that would bring us across the Atlantic to Boston.

The Architect and his wife came to pick us up in a Fiat. He commented on how silent I was during the car ride from the airport to his home. Was I not excited to be in America? Did I not feel amazed to ride through a tunnel that was built under sea level? What did I think of escalators? The luggage conveyor belt? The crisp New England weather? Did I like the taste of Schweppes ginger ale? I was silent because I was tired. I was always eager to provide the correct answer to questions posed by adults. In America, however, children are not always quizzed by adults looking to extract the correct answer; sometimes they are asked about their feelings. So I worried about what my correct feeling should be in each circumstance.

The Architect already had a small rental apartment lined up for us. It was located within a modest three-story wooden house on a little street that sat on the border between rich Cambridge and its poorer neighbor, Somerville. The house was owned by Harvard; and the university, acting as landlord, rented it to a variety of people, even those without university connections. On the first floor lived a Spaniard who was studying for a PhD at MIT. He owned a

Porsche. I was told it was a very expensive car. On the second floor lived a single white American woman who worked as a bartender. On weekends she cooked a roast that made the entire house, from attic to basement, stink. On the third floor lived a graduate student of religion. He had just finished his doctorate at Harvard and was about to leave for a new job at a prestigious small college nearby. It was his two-bedroom apartment that we were going to rent from the university real estate office. Baba said the apartment was "romantic." That was the first time I heard him use that word. To me, it was an unusual space full of wildly sloping roofs, odd closets within closets (the previous tenant had, for purposes known only to him, built closets within walk-in closets and covered the floors of those interior closets with wall-to-wall shag carpeting). The bathroom was tiny and the roof sloped so steeply that it was impossible to stand in the bathtub. The ceiling was so low on one side of my parents' bedroom that you had to roll out of the bed carefully to avoid bumping your head.

The kitchen had a white lace curtain, left behind no doubt by the student of religion. It seemed like something only people who live in rich countries do—leave behind such beautiful things like a lace curtain. He also left behind a set of blue melamine dinner plates with a cluster of flowers in the center of each plate. The plates had a set of matching blue melamine bowls. In the freezer, he left a tub of Brigham's strawberry ice cream. It was still half-full. We ate that ice cream during our first few nights in the apartment, awed by the wealth of a country where one could leave behind half a tub of delicious and perfectly edible ice cream with such careless largesse.

Before we moved to our own attic apartment, we stayed with the Architect and his wife for a week. During this period, we acquired all necessary paperwork for beginning life in the United States. We all received our Social Security cards. My parents learned how to use the T, Boston's public transportation system. The Architect's wife taught Ma how to use washing machines and vacuum cleaners, and how to cook using American-style ovens. We were taken to supermarkets by our hosts and shown where to buy food and household products. We were used to Indian bazaars with butchers, fishmongers, vegetable sellers all hawking their goods in a cacophonous, open-air, slippery, wet environment that smelled of fish scales and offal and chicken feathers and vegetables still covered in dirt from the farm. Each vendor, for eggs, fish, goat meat, fruit, loose tea leaves, and so forth, had his own specialty and developed a relationship with his long-term customers. Everyone bargained vociferously. The milkman, who owned his own cow, brought milk in an aluminum pail every morning. Our neighborhood butcher had seen me since I was a toddler and always saved for us the parts of a goat—ears, kidneys, marrow bones—that he knew I relished. In Calcutta, almost everyone shopped daily for food, in modest quantities. A hushed, brightly lit supermarket where families loaded their carts with a month's worth of groceries was a new experience for us.

The Architect had notified his vast network of our arrival, so we found many cardboard boxes filled with bed linens, towels, dishes, pots and pans, old clothes, and outdated, bulky winter coats (because everyone knew that a new family from Calcutta was unlikely to be prepared for New England snow). I was taken to the Cambridge Public School Department's main office and after a few hours of looking through my old school report cards, the school officials decided that I would be placed in the seventh grade at the Peabody School, located in one of Cambridge's more affluent neighborhoods. Our apartment was not in this neighborhood. So, the same officials also decided that I would take the school bus daily.

• • •

August 11, 1982. That was my Arrival Day. My detailed recollection of that day and the ensuing weeks has an unexpected historical parallel. Indians had arrived in the New World long before the U.S. immigration laws were reconfigured in 1965. Thousands of Indians arrived in the New World in the early nineteenth century. They traveled on slave ships and disembarked in places with names such as Port-of-Spain or Georgetown.

The majority of these Indians embarked on ships from

Hooghly Harbor, in the city of Calcutta. I had already encountered their descendants when I was a girl. When I saw
those blurry images of black West Indian cricketers in the
Statesman I also saw photos of Indian players standing
next to them. Alvin Kallicharran. Rohan Kanhai. These
men with subcontinental names played for the West Indies.
Through cricket matches we caught a glimpse of our vast
diaspora.

When slavery was abolished in the British Empire during the 1830s, plantation owners in the Caribbean feared
that a labor vacuum would affect the production of sugar.
Vast profits were to be made from Caribbean sugar in the
nineteenth century and many wealthy British families were
involved in the business. As newly freed Afro-Creole slaves
moved from the plantations to the cities, the British started
looking for alternate sources of labor. After some experimentation with other populations—Scots, Lebanese, Syri-
ans, Palestinians, Chinese—they arrived at the conclusion
that villagers recruited from the Indo-Gangetic Plain were
best suited to cultivating sugarcane. This was no mere hap-
penstance. These Indian farmers were already cultivating
sugarcane in their villages. India, as recorded history tells
us, was producing refined sugar before Alexander the Great
arrived in Punjab in the fourth century BCE. A few decades
later, in his book *Indika*, the Greek ethnographer Megas-
thenes described the sugarcane plants of India as reeds that
bear honey without the aid of bees.

Since their empire stretched from Guyana in South America to Hong Kong in Asia, the British had easy access to Indian sugarcane farmers. They were subjects who could be moved around the globe according to the needs of the rulers. These Indians were brought to the New World as indentured laborers to work in the same cane fields where black slaves had toiled for centuries. The indentured laborers lived in the slave barracks. They traveled on board the same ships that had been used in the slave trade. Indentured laborers—derisively called "coolies"—were not slaves before the eyes of the law. But can we call them immigrants? These men and women did sign an agreement—indentureship papers—and were looking for higher wages and better employment opportunities. Can we call them *Homo economicus*? Did they make a rational choice to journey perilously on board old slave ships—a journey that often proved fatal? Did they know what conditions awaited them in the New World? Did they know most of them would never return after their period of indentureship concluded?

What we do know is that these Indians called themselves *girmityas*. It is a beautiful instance of an English word that has been appropriated and indigenized by Indians to great aesthetic and political ends. The English word "agreement"—referring to the indentureship contract—is the foundation of *girmit*. *Girmityas* is the plural form of the noun. *Girmityas* make up most of the global labor diaspora of South Asians. From Fiji to Uganda to Trinidad, *girmityas* built infrastructure, grew cash crops, and generated wealth for the British Empire. The men who are building the Louvre and the Guggenheim in Abu Dhabi are the modern-day *girmityas*. The Indian men who bus tables in hole-in-the-wall curry joints in London, or the Indian women who work as domestic help in American suburbs, are following the footsteps of *girmityas*.

White-collar, graduate-school-educated, Indian STEM professionals who have immigrated to the United States since the 1990s see themselves as unrelated to these contemporary coolies, or to *girmityas* of another era. What does an Ivy-educated Silicon Valley entrepreneur who has just raised millions of dollars for his start-up have in common with the illiterate sugarcane farmer who has just stepped off the ship in Port-of-Spain, Trinidad, in 1838? Perhaps not much, but our older diasporas in the southern Caribbean might have a few pertinent lessons to offer us. Lessons in living with people of other races, in politics, in Americanization, and in creolization.

Americanization to me is a New World phenomenon—a phenomenon of the Americas. Americanization is something far more profound than simple assimilation into the dominant culture of the United States. It is a process of creolization. The English *creole*, the Spanish *criollo*, the French *créole*, the Portuguese *crioulo*—all these words have a common root in the Latin *creare*, to produce or create. The creole is born in the New World. Even more expansively, we can say that *the creole is created in the New World.* In this sense, all immigrants are creole. Indeed, all of the Americas is creole. The creole is the most valuable thing made in America.

Some creoles celebrate arrival on American shores and others celebrate emancipation from slavery on American shores. My memory of August 11, 1982, is a precious relic. As each year takes me further away from the moment of arrival, I polish and preserve my relic with religious zeal. During the month of May each year—May 30 in the island nation of Trinidad and Tobago, and May 5 in Guyana—Indian arrival is celebrated with great fanfare by the descendants of indentured laborers. The descendants of slaves, the Afro-Creole population of the Caribbean, do not celebrate their own Arrival Day. Can you imagine celebrating the arrival of your ancestors in shackles on board slave ships? What would that parade look like? On the first day of August each year, the black citizens of Trinidad and Guyana celebrate Emancipation Day.

Those who celebrate arrival and those who celebrate emancipation—what is the distance between these two groups? For one the sense of belonging in the New World is rooted in the triumph of arrival. For another the sense of belonging in the New World is rooted in the tragedy of enslavement. These are two threads of world history, two threads of racial memory, two ways of looking at how we came to be here.

When I was a young academic doing research in the

Caribbean I began to see my memory of arrival—a memory that Ma, Baba, and I kept alive in our home through frequent retellings—as part of the story of large population movements. This story was far bigger in scope, involving millions of actors, thousands of species of flora and fauna, hundreds of years, and vast sums of money, and spanning the world from the Ganges River to the Caribbean Sea.

* * *

I arrived in Boston during the Reagan years. The Cold War was on. The Berlin Wall stood tall. India was a nonaligned Third World nation of little consequence to the United States. It was long before the era of cell phones and social media. In the last century—the era of aerogrammes and trunk calls in India—for those in economically straitened circumstances the imagination was the best possible mobile device for conjuring up a home left behind. I missed our little one-bedroom home in Calcutta, my school, my neighborhood. I remembered Darwanji, who had taken me for walks since I was a toddler. I imagined the cows that slept on the sidewalk outside our main door, the feral dogs that barked all night, the harsh sound of the crows. The silence of the American streets made me homesick. At first, each season brought unfamiliar sensations. When I walked to the bus stop or to the laundromat with Ma, everyone seemed to be inside their house doing things I did not quite understand. And a little part of me felt humiliated—even though

I did not know how to give a name and shape to that shame—that my parents had to leave the country of my birth for economic reasons. I cried into my pillow and in locked bathrooms. I craved the food we ate every day back in India, even though before we left I had not thought it was anything special. I yearned to speak in my mother tongue everywhere I went.

The Architect gave me my first American book. It was called *The Stranger* and was written by a man whose name I read in my mind as Kamooose but was told by my benefactor—a childless man who mercifully did not give me reading-grade-appropriate books—that I was pronouncing the author's name incorrectly. I did not like the book but read diligently because it made me sad to read about a man whose mother had died and who went to jail and there was no happy ending. It matched my own unnameable mood. The novel was in English—though upon later inspection I found it had not been written in English originally. I wanted to make sure my English was very good because I had overheard my parents worrying that my language skills may not be up to snuff for American schools. My shimmering linguistic world of Bengali now shrunk to the confines of our little attic apartment furnished largely with things others had discarded.

When people move they inevitably bring certain things with them, leave a few things behind, and acquire new possessions. My parents had asked me to choose what I wanted to take with me to Boston. I was allotted a single suitcase.

Everything else was to be sold, given to relatives, or thrown away. This is what I chose to bring in my suitcase:

Red plastic View-Master with four reels (Disney World, Japan, Baby Animals, and Mecca)

Four Bengali books—*Raj Kahini* (Royal Tales) by Abanindranath Tagore; *Aam Antir Bhepu* (The Song of the Road) by Bibhutibhushan Bandyopadhyay; *Shishu* (Child), a collection of poems by Rabindranath Tagore; and *Gopal Bhand* (Stories of Gopal the Royal Fool)

My report cards from my old school, attesting to my grades from 1974 to 1982

My beloved collection of miniature plastic animals that came free with the purchase of Binaca brand toothpaste in India during the 1970s

A Misha commemorative pin from the 1980 Moscow Olympics

A couple of dresses made of printed cotton

A pair of gray denim pants, the closest thing I owned to the coveted American blue jeans

A pair of blue canvas shoes from Bata, the most
popular shoe company in India

None of these items were going to be of much practi-
cal use, as I soon found out. The tools and weapons I
needed to survive and flourish in the New World were
waiting for me elsewhere. I would find them in the hall-
ways of my new school. And on the small screen of our
black-and-white TV.

At my new school on Linnaean Street, I soon found
out, we had no uniforms and all classes were coeducational. I learned that when the teacher calls on you in
an American class, you do not stand up to answer. My
American teachers always asked for our opinions about
everything we were studying—history, literature, science,
mathematics, programming in BASIC. I was accustomed to
memorizing everything and regurgitating it during tests.
That was the Indian way of succeeding in school. I had
done well in my Calcutta school precisely because I had a
good memory and could learn everything by heart. What
use was by-heart learning when a teacher asked for my
opinion? Much like answering questions about my feelings,
I was baffled by having to offer my opinion on the subjects
we studied in class. In those early days, I marveled at the
confidence with which some of my American classmates—
many of whom were far behind me in subjects such as
math, science, and history—expressed their opinions on

everything with great clarity, and even challenged the teacher on occasion.

At my old school, each class (what Americans called "grade") had sections (what Americans called "home-rooms"). At my old school, no teacher attempted to entertain the students. School was serious business. In order to make school more joyful, everything at the Peabody School was given a funny name. My school bus was called the Red Lobster and bore a small image of the crustacean on its windshield. Homerooms had names inspired by classic 1980s arcade games—Asteroids, Defenders, Omega Race. I was a member of Omega Race—absolutely clueless about arcades or the game itself.

In Indian schools there were no cafeterias, so everyone brought their own lunch in tiffin boxes. We ate our tiffin at our desk or while wandering about the school corridors or out in the playground during tiffin time. Americans have recess and school lunches are served in cafeterias. Sloppy joes, Salisbury steaks, chicken nuggets, square pizzas, Jell-O, endless small cartons of milk. My classmates zipped through the cafeteria line, long familiar with the menu and confident in their own preferences. I had a lot of catching up to do.

The Peabody School was located in a white, upper-middle-class neighborhood. Most of the black and Hispanic students traveled by school buses from other neighborhoods. During class, we had assigned seating. During recess, however, most students self-segregated according to race. It did not take a long time for a young immigrant girl to notice this. I had to learn where I should sit at lunch and who I should expect to hang out with at recess. Our apartment was not close to the school. After school it was not possible for me to walk over to the beautiful homes of those classmates who lived a block or two away. None of them asked me over anyway. Other kids—mostly black, Hispanic, and a few Asian ones—climbed into school buses and disappeared to different parts of town. At the time, I did not know that the entire city of Boston had been embroiled in a school desegregation battle that had pitted white families against black families since the controversial 1965 Massachusetts Racial Imbalance Act. In the early 1980s, the dust had not quite settled yet. The headline-grabbing riots of the 1970s were over—the wars in which white families from South Boston and Charlestown refused federally mandated desegregation of schools through busing; the wars in which white and black students were beaten up by those who opposed their political views. The word "desegregation" was never spoken out loud by anyone inside my school. Occasionally, I heard the mysterious word "busing" mentioned by the teachers but had no idea what they meant by it.

Except for our black gym teacher, all my teachers at the Peabody School were white. The principal was white.

Everyone who worked in the principal's office was white. I was not adept enough at parsing American surnames. Unless a teacher spoke at length about his family, I could not yet tell the difference between an Irish American and an Armenian American, between a Jew and a WASP. I did not understand that all Christians were not on equal footing. As a Hindu girl who was educated by nuns for most of her life up to that point, Catholicism and Christianity were inseparable for me. I had attended a Christian school in Calcutta. Naming it as "Catholic" would be as strange to me as labeling the followers of Jesus in the tenth century as "Catholics." Weren't all Christians Catholics? The first Protestants I encountered at close quarters lived in Cambridge. They belonged to a dizzying variety of denominations and churches. While being wholly ignorant of the religious history of America, I was beginning to sense that there were hierarchies among white Christians. It felt like sitting down at someone else's family dinner table midway through a meal. Old quarrels echoed in the polite tinkling of silverware as everyone ate in silence.

I would have to wait two more years, until I started high school, when blacks and Asians would be my teachers. Yet, already I sensed there were fault lines within our Omega Race. My black classmates sat in their own groups in the cafeteria, huddled together between classes, wore their clothes in slightly different styles. In Calcutta, I knew that I must not speak with Prakash when he walked into a room.

In Cambridge, I did not yet know the rules of silence among children. A hurricane had blown through Boston and its surrounds in the decade preceding my arrival. I found the detritus all around me but had no idea how to decode it.

In the early 1980s, Asians and Latinos were caught between Boston's black and white polarized politics. Many Asians and Latinos opposed desegregation of the schools for their own reasons. The Chinese and Latino communities, for instance, had worked hard to form public bilingual schools in the city during the 1970s and desegregation would jeopardize the existence of such schools. Meanwhile, the arrival of new immigrants from Southeast Asia, following America's disastrous war in the region, was fanning the flames of anti-Asian sentiments in working-class white neighborhoods. Indian immigrants like me were still relatively rare in Boston. The real wave of arrivals would start almost a decade later, during the 1990s, as H-1B visas would be used by companies to bring temporary Indian workers who could be paid much less than native-born American IT professionals.

Aged twelve, I knew very little about the desegregation wars being fought in city halls and in public schools. I knew very little about the changing demographics of Boston as new kinds of immigrants were beginning to change the face and the politics of the city. What I did know was that I had to devise a plan for Total Americanization before the end of the year.

⁕ ⁕ ⁕

Between Labor Day 1982 and Christmas 1982, I was determined to acquire a new American accent. I did this by watching a lot of shows after school on a nine-inch black-and-white Sony TV, handed down to us by the Architect. *General Hospital, Hawaii Five-O, Happy Days, Laverne & Shirley, Three's Company, The Jeffersons, Good Times*—I watched it all after school when I was alone at home. There was no one to guide me through the maze of different eras of American culture, different regions, classes, or even races being depicted in these shows. I swallowed the whole lot in one voracious bite.

Playing with the channel knob of that old television, I had chanced upon the ABC soap *General Hospital* early in the autumn of 1982. *General Hospital* aired at three p.m. EST, which worked perfectly with my schedule. I would quickly walk home from the school bus stop, let myself into our attic apartment, grab an Entenmann's frosted chocolate doughnut, and sit on the floor in front of the TV screen. Since we'd never had a TV before, I did not mind that I could not see all of Port Charles, the fictional setting of *GH*, in full color. In black and white, Edward and Lila Quartermaine quarreled in their mansion. Nurses gossiped in their station. Robert Scorpio chased criminals on behalf of the WSB, an international spy agency. Frisco romanced Felicia. The young

Demi Moore, John Stamos, Ricky Martin, and Rick Springfield all entered my life in black and white. I was addicted.

The British actress Emma Samms played the role of
Holly, the love interest of Robert Scorpio played by the Aus-
tralian actor Tristan Rogers. Holly fascinated me. I wanted
her perm, her clothes, her life. Later, when Holly left the
show, Anna Devane—played by another British actress,
Finola Hughes—became my new ideal. What attracted me
to these characters—Robert, Anna, and Holly, and later,
the character of Jax played by Ingo Rademacher—was their
desirable foreignness. They lived in the all-American Port
Charles but carried marks of their outsider status as Brits or
Aussies. They spoke English with a different accent. If only
I could be different like them. The sort of foreigner with an
accent that Americans love, not the sort of foreigner who is
teased for sounding funny.

Even the villainous Cassadines possessed a type of foreignness that I lacked. They were Russian aristocrats with
their own Greek island. They had cool names such as Hel-
ena, Stavros, and Nikolas. Sharmila never sounded like the
name of a person who might own a Greek island. Port
Charles, as I knew it back then, was largely white. Occasionally a mobster like Sonny Corinthos showed up with
hints of vague brownness. But Sonny's Cuban, Greek, and
Italian background really did not make much sense to me.

On early-release days, I watched all the other ABC

soaps on Channel 5. This became familiar American geography to me—Pine Valley, PA. Llanview, PA. Corinth, PA. Port Charles, NY. If I did not understand all the cultural references or the colloquialisms at first, by the end of my first twelve months in the United States, I was fluent in the language of American soaps.

Before my parents came home from work, I had two to three hours of viewing freedom. From Port Charles, New York, I wandered to other places. I peeked into different American homes, trying to break the code and learn the rules of engagement. The rural Virginia home on Walton's Mountain was nothing like the Chicago apartment of *Good Times*. Florida and James's financial struggles looked different from those of John and Olivia. With little knowledge about the Great Depression of the 1930s or the Cabrini-Green projects of inner-city Chicago during the 1970s, watching these slices of American life was like playing with a heap of jigsaw puzzle pieces without the complete image on the box to guide me. It takes a lot longer to put the pieces together this way. Sometimes a small fragment of the puzzle comes together, while the larger picture continues to be elusive.

Why did J.J. act like a buffoon and keep saying "dy-no-mite!" when his parents were always overworked and stressed? Why was J.J. not as wise and thoughtful as John-Boy Walton? I understood that all would end well for the Walton family. The adult John-Boy's calm voice-over was proof that the future was going to be rosier than the present. But what future lay in store for the Evans family? Despite J.J.'s goofiness, I sensed the jagged edges of desperation inside Florida's home. Ma, Baba, and I lived with similar jagged edges in our attic apartment.

Little did I know that I was watching old reruns. *The Waltons* and *Good Times* had been canceled a few years prior to my arrival. My experience with television in Calcutta was limited to the occasional show I saw in a neighbor's home. India had one channel in that era—Doordarshan—and it was state-run. Its broadcast hours were limited. In Cambridge, I could barely believe my own good fortune that we finally possessed our own TV and it came with six or seven local channels. Reruns, sitcoms, daytime soaps, nighttime dramas, miniseries, talk shows, game shows, spin-offs, season finales, series finales—I was becoming proficient in American TV talk. Sometimes I looked at the *TV Guide* on display at the supermarket in order to decode the complex program schedules. My parents never subscribed to *TV Guide*. Instead, they subscribed to *Reader's Digest* and *Better Homes & Gardens*.

Dynasty taught me how American rich people live. *Three's Company* taught me how American roommates behave. *Welcome Back, Kotter* taught me how American high schools work. *Solid Gold* taught me how Americans dance. *The Jeffersons* taught me that having a piece of the pie meant movin' on up to the East Side to a deluxe apartment in the sky. I had a crush on Vinnie Barbarino of the Sweathogs. I wished I had blond hair like Krystle Carrington. The young anthropologist among natives was Going Native herself. I was assimilating.

Then, out of the blue one day, our social studies teacher announced we were going on a field trip to see a movie.

The entire seventh grade class went to see Richard Attenborough's *Gandhi*. Ben Kingsley played the lead role. Ben Kingsley, as I later discovered, is the stage name of the biracial British actor Krishna Bhanji. I had to endure over three hours of seeing Kingsley as a mystical Gandhi lecturing the British about the evils of their empire. I hated Gandhi's comical accent in the movie. I cringed in the darkened movie theater as Kingsley racebent his way through the movie, wearing brown body paint and the skimpiest of loincloths.

The inevitable jokes followed when we returned to school. Everyone started mimicking the accent they'd heard in the film. They asked me if I rode to school on elephants. Someone even asked me if I wore a grass skirt in India, confusing one tropical stereotype for another. They asked me if my father dressed as Gandhi did. Our well-meaning social studies teacher beamed at me during classes over the next few weeks as he lectured us on how Gandhi's nonviolent techniques influenced the American Civil Rights Movement. The teacher kept on looking at me each time Gandhi was mentioned and called on me more frequently than usual. *Sharmila, tell us something about civil disobedience. Sharmila, tell us about Mahatma Gandhi.* I imagined I heard whispers and titters from the back of the class. I imagined my American classmates saying, *Yeah, tell us why your great leader was so skinny and why he was half-naked all the time. Tell us why you guys talk so funny. Tell us if you come from a place crowded with so many dark, poor people.*

I detested Attenborough's India. White adults loved the movie. That made me hate it even more. Everyone said Attenborough showed India on film for the first time. I wanted to scream that I had seen hundreds of films that showed me India—Hindi movies, Bengali movies. I missed those movies now. My glorious American television set had only one flaw. It did not feature Hindi films. I barely saw anyone Indian on our TV screen when we arrived.

In 1982, Kal Penn and Mindy Kaling had not even started kindergarten. Aziz Ansari and Lilly Singh were yet to be born. My three children see Priyanka Chopra's face featured in advertisements for *Quantico* on the sides of buses these days. They follow Superwoman and Humble the Poet on YouTube. If you were a brown kid thirty years ago in the United States as I was, you knew it was pointless to look for someone resembling you on-screen—not just resembling you in complexion, but actually representing your reality, your plotlines. Brown people appeared rarely in leading roles. When we did get a bit part, we were always straitjacketed into narrow types. Occasionally, I caught a glimpse of Kabir Bedi on *General Hospital* and a flash of Persis Khambatta in *Star Trek*. I had to wait until the 1990s to see names like Naveen Andrews and Sarita Choudhury on credit rolls. Then came Aziz Ansari, Dr. Sanjay Gupta, Mindy Kaling, Hasan Minhaj, Parminder Nagra, Archie Panjabi, and Kal Penn.

Once Ma and I went to see a movie about the life of the Buddha. After the movie was over, she said, "Who was that handsome Indian boy who played the Buddha? I haven't seen him before. Is he a new actor from Bombay?"

"Ma," I responded, "that wasn't an Indian boy. That was Keanu Reeves in brownface."

We both walked out of the movie theater a little dejected. In the 1990s, even the Buddha was whitewashed on the American screen.

Guest appearances, part of a large ensemble cast—that was all we got in America for a while. There was one tiny exception, however. While playing with the channel knob, Ma and I discovered a local TV channel that broadcast an Indian variety program on weekends. It was hosted by a woman named Vimi Verma. Once a week, for thirty minutes, she returned us to the world of movies and songs we had left behind. My parents and I scheduled our weekends around this program. It was wonderful to hear Hindi words coming out of the TV, and to see scenes from old

Hindi movies. Somewhere, we sensed, there were others like us in the United States. They too worked in American offices, wore American clothes, shopped in American supermarkets. But they missed the movies of Rajesh Khanna and Sharmila Tagore, of Dharmendra and Hema Malini, of Amitabh Bachchan and Rekha. Cable TV had not yet brought hundreds of channels from all over the world into American homes. Moreover, we could not have afforded a cable subscription back then in any case. We were content to watch the staticky screen and relish those beloved films. Fiddling with the radio dial, Ma came across a program hosted by a man named Harish Dang. Every weekend, Harish Dang played Hindi film songs on his program. When my parents saved enough money to buy a tape recorder, Ma diligently taped those songs directly from the radio and started building her own library of homemade Hindi film song cassettes. After work, when Ma had finished cooking and tidying up, she would play those songs over and over again. It was our way of creating a small familiar space inside our new country. It was our DIY All India Radio.

We would have to wait a few more years before Ma and Baba had saved some more money to buy a VCR. I waited eagerly for the day when we would have our own VCR. I did not want to watch Hollywood movies on it. Despite all my attempts at Total Americanization, I still craved Hindi films. As soon as we bought that VCR, Ma and I started trekking out to Indian grocery stores in Central Square that rented VHS tapes of Hindi movies. Often these tapes were of terrible quality. They were pirated copies made by entrepreneurial Indians who knew that homesickness would make their customers forgive the fuzzy pictures and bad sound quality.

I kept all this a secret from my new friends at school. I did not think they would understand my need to watch Bollywood movies. Outside the home, I listened to the latest cool music. The Police, Pet Shop Boys, Fine Young Cannibals, Spandau Ballet, Tears for Fears, Roxy Music, Robert Palmer, Sade. I was going through an eighties British pop phase. I walked to Newbury Comics after school and looked at fanzines with my white friends. We talked about the latest records and the cutest new singers. At home, I spoke in Bengali and listened to Hindi music tapes. I built a secret palace for the Indian me inside my mind. A palace furnished with memories of another country and fueled by homemade cassette tapes and pirated videos.

Once I had watched Hindi movies in crowded Calcutta cinema halls. Now I watched Hindi movies behind closed doors with Ma and Baba. I avoided speaking Bengali in public. I ate with my fingers only at our family table. I was changing into something else. For the first time, I saw myself as a minority, a person of color. I did not like it.

· · ·

I do not think my three children, all born in the long shadow of 9/11, will be able to recollect a time when they did not know that words such as minority, non-white, non-Christian, South Asian were meant to designate them. Our eldest child—a daughter whom we adopted—was born in New Delhi. Before she received her immigration papers from the U.S. embassy, we had to sign a form assuring the American government that our five-month-old baby was not a terrorist. Our youngest son was born in Boston and had already missed a few flights before he was six because his name, Kabir Singh, used to appear on no-fly lists. That Kabir is no longer stopped in airports, I assume, is because somewhere a computer has learned his year of birth—2005.

Perhaps some of the half million or more people who immigrated to the United States in 1982 also got race the way I did. Looking at those statistics now, I feel deep comfort. I was never alone. Yet, I felt very lonely at the time, desperately trying to mimic the correct American accent by watching *General Hospital* and *Hawaii Five-O*. To be the foreign kid with an odd-sounding name was no fun in the public school classrooms. Kids with foreign accents and strange-smelling lunches would be teased mercilessly. So I, along with the other foreign kids who were new to our school that year, decided to speak like "real Americans" as quickly as possible. Changing one's accent, however, does not lead to immediate acceptance by American public school kids, themselves in the midst of a historic experiment in racial integration in the city of Boston. Who was I going to be in this society? I would soon find out. I would have to spell my name for everyone. My surname, which once carried a surfeit of information about me, would become empty of meaning. And then I would be remade, imbued with new meaning. I would speak with an American accent, pretend my mother roasted a turkey for Thanksgiving, try to understand Judy Blume characters, decide whether I preferred Duran Duran or Run DMC, and figure out whether I should sit with the white kids, the black kids, or the Hispanic kids during lunch in the school cafeteria. I sat, in the end, with a ragtag group of foreign kids.

Mimicry is a handy skill to have when you are an alien. I copied everything. Gestures, pauses between words, facial expressions, intonations. A small mistake could set me back in my journey into assimilation. If the native-born kids in school were like the Borg from *Star Trek*, I was that rare species that offered no resistance whatsoever to assimilation. Go ahead and put your nanoprobes into me quickly, I would tell them. You don't need to tell me resistance is futile. I have no intention of resisting.

Speaking American Like I Wasn't Trying Too Hard required months of hard work, carried out in secret. In this activity, I had a close friend and ally—another foreigner. A girl from Naples had arrived at our school the year before— the daughter of a Neapolitan physicist and a Scottish nurse. My Italian friend also believed in using television as an educational device for Total Americanization. Since English was not our mother tongue we were exquisitely alert to every nuance, every variation, every slang used by the natives. When we were not practicing our English, my friend would tell me of her life in Naples, about the island of Capri and a magical place called Pompeii. She taught me a song about a beautiful parrot. I tried to mimic her way of pronouncing those words because she told me she missed hearing vowels and consonants pronounced as it once was in her native country.

> *Come è bello pappagallo*
> *Tutto rosso,*
> *Verde, giallo.*
> *Cosa fai?*
> *Dove vai?*
> *Come è bello pappagaaaaaaaallo.*

I never taught her any songs in my mother tongue. I felt ashamed to speak Bengali in front of classmates in the Peabody School. Soon our group was rounded off by another foreign girl, though she had spent too many years in Cambridge to be truly called "foreign." Her parents had emigrated from Hong Kong. She spoke Mandarin at home and was raised according to strict, aristocratic Chinese norms. When I visited her home, located in a wealthy neighborhood in Cambridge, I was awed by the elegant living room filled with beautiful objects from faraway China. Her mother always carried an expensive leather handbag, and I spied lotions made by a company called Shiseido in their medicine cabinet. The three of us—a Chinese, an Italian, and an Indian—forged our own ties within a school where the dominant racial groups could not quite accommodate us. At the end of every school day, each of us went home to eat food that would be strange to most of our classmates.

·   ·   ·

Ma, meanwhile, faced a different problem. In the early 1980s, Indian grocery stores were mostly located in distant Boston suburbs where the nascent Indian immigrant community lived. We did not own a car and reaching these stores was nearly impossible. In the Star Market near our apartment, Ma found some turmeric and a few sticks of cinnamon in Durkee jars. She found rice and some lentils. The rest she would have to improvise. Ma had dropped out of college at nineteen to marry the brother of one of her classmates. Until she arrived in the United States, she had been a Bengali housewife. Now she had a part-time job in a Harvard library (soon to be turned into a full-time job).

During the day, she shed her usual sari, wore hand-me-down trousers and blouses, and walked to an office where she would have to converse in English. She managed with smiles and gestures when her wobbly English failed her. In the evenings, she tried to transform American supermarket chicken into something resembling a Bengali *murgir jhol*, a chicken curry. Soon Baba would start returning home—frustrated, angry, tired—demanding that we eat "American food" instead of our improvised Indian meals.

I will never know for sure what happened to him in his new job. The clothing shop sold very expensive men's suits for Boston Brahmins. It was owned by an Armenian American and the tailors who did the alterations upstairs were recent immigrants from Italy. Sales were handled by an Irish American and an Italian. It was and continues to be a very elite, white, male store. A stone's throw from Harvard Yard, the store dressed the most successful WASPs of the city and was run by white men who did not possess Ivy League degrees and were never allowed into the club themselves. In 1982, add to this volatile mixture an Indian man. None of them had worked closely with an Indian before, or been to India. Their knowledge of Indian food was limited to the one or two curry restaurants dotting the Central Square area of Cambridge. Often Baba would come home from work, after a day-long tutorial on the merits of the two-button, side-vented jacket, or after mastering a proper four-in-hand, a half Windsor, or a full Windsor, and repeat the lines he had heard at work from his coworkers. "Cumin smells like armpits." "Cilantro is revolting." Suddenly, *jeera* and *dhania*—cumin and coriander, the beloved staples of an Indian spice box—became offensive.

Thus began our great experiment in "American cuisine," which we really understood to mean "white people's food." While I was scanning every entry in the 1968 edition of the *World Book Encyclopedia*, a set we had bought for a few pennies at a yard sale, Ma began looking for recipes on the backs of boxes and cans. Bisquick boxes and Campbell's soup cans were especially helpful. All sorts of tasty casseroles and baked items could be created by adding Campbell's mushroom soup or some powdered Bisquick mix to prosaic, cheap ingredients. Because we thought white people always had a soup course, we started each dinner with soup. Ma found that ramen noodle packets sold ten for a dollar. We shared one ramen noodle packet, ladled into three blue melamine bowls, at the start of each dinner at our kitchen table (there was no separate dining room table). We ate our meals with spoons, forks, and knives, Western-style. The soup was followed by broccoli and chicken, bathed in Campbell's condensed mushroom soup, covered in Kraft shredded cheddar cheese, and baked in the oven. Jell-O was a frequent dessert. It was also cheap. Our supermarket cart in those days contained things like cans of Spam, the cheapest brand of baloney, squishy white bread, Kraft cheddar cheese, Little Debbie snack cakes, Entenmann's doughnuts, lots of Campbell's soups, Bisquick, Jell-O, Cool Whip, and dozens of packages of ramen noodles.

E. M. Forster once wrote that the English in India ate the food of exiles cooked by natives who did not understand it. We, a newly arrived immigrant family, ate what we thought was the food of Americans and cooked without understanding it. General Mills and the Campbell's Soup Company were our local guides. And we stopped eating our own food, which we did understand, for a while, because someone had taunted Baba by saying cumin smelled of armpits.

White people's food seemed to come in three colors—green, red, and white. Salads were green. Salads were also new to us. Though we ate a wide variety of vegetables in Calcutta, raw vegetables were rarely served as anything other than a garnish. My palate was unaccustomed to something as exotic as a bowl of raw lettuce drizzled with a pungent, unctuous liquid. Once I was served this kind of a dish with small cubes of toasted bread, pieces of bland chicken, and a few tiny fish. It was called a chicken Caesar salad. I found it revolting. We never ate chicken that was not marinated in at least four types of spices and grilled in a clay oven or braised in a curry. I grew up in a rice-and-fish culture, but the anchovies were hard to stomach. We were freshwater fish eaters. Salmon and cod did not suit our tastes.

The red foods were pizzas and pastas. These were easier on my palate, but it still took me the greater part of two years to appreciate oregano. I might have been an aficionado of the *masala dabba*, the Indian spice box, but I was scared of new spices from other lands. The white foods were easiest to like. Mac and cheese, Ma's casseroles doused in Campbell's condensed mushroom soup, grilled cheese sandwiches—it required relatively little effort to develop a taste for such food.

Most of what Ma cooked included processed food. Bits and pieces from cans, boxes, and packets. These packages were beautiful. In Calcutta, our kitchen larder rarely had so many brightly labeled cans and boxes. Processed foods would invade Indian homes from the 1990s onward, after liberalization of the economy enabled foreign brands to penetrate the Indian market. There are two American dishes that Ma made from scratch during our first years that stand out in our family's collective memory. The Architect's wife taught Ma how to bake macaroni and cheese using freshly grated white cheddar, cream, and lots of butter. The cheesy elbow macaroni, topped with golden bread crumbs, was easily one of our new family favorites. The other dish was saved for weekends and special occasions. Ma had become friends with an older black woman in her office. Enid used to bring a date nut bread, her signature dessert, to office potlucks and one day she wrote down the recipe for Ma. I will always remember Enid's date nut bread as the first American dessert we learned to bake from scratch.

Enid told Ma that the bread had to be baked in an old coffee can. I marveled at her ingenuity because when the dark brown bread slid out of that coffee can it was shaped like a fat cylinder, complete with tiny ridges around the middle. Ma and I followed Enid's recipe carefully. Dates were chopped precisely. The walnuts were broken into small pieces. We used brown sugar, never white sugar. The Folgers coffee can was greased liberally with butter. After the cake came out, we served it with softened Philadelphia cream cheese. I had tasted nothing like this in Calcutta. We would not have learned the coffee can trick, grasped the importance of brown sugar, or discovered that tangy, salty cream cheese pairs so well with a sweet bread, if it was not for Enid's generosity. Hers was the first recipe we received in writing when we came to America. Now I realize that it was a bit of American cultural memory, written down and shared with a newcomer.

Outside the home, I continued eating American with halting fluency. Hamburger meat smelled too beefy to a girl who had eaten well-spiced goat meat most of her life. The skin on fried chicken revolted me because we did not eat poultry with its skin intact in Calcutta. Rare steak was beyond our reach financially, but I could not imagine eating something that still bled. The oregano and basil in pizza sauce were always too strong for me. I could never finish an entire can of soda because I was unaccustomed to such large portions. The Architect attempted to show us how wealthy white people ate, people who had degrees from Harvard, tasteful furniture, walls lined with bookshelves, and jobs that carried prestige. He introduced us to sushi, sashimi, miso soup, goose liver pâté, smoked salmon, blue cheese, Mestemacher rye bread, and granola. He introduced us to farms in Lexington and told us that it was fashionable to buy produce from farms, not from Star Market. He told us not to put too much salt on our food because that betrayed our lack of sophistication. He told us not to overcook the vegetables or the pasta. Sophisticated white Americans ate everything slightly undersalted and undercooked. We gamely tried all these new foods with the Architect. Then, at home, we reverted to ramen, cheap baloney, and Little Debbie.

The Architect bought me my first candied apple. He took us to Café Pamplona on Bow Street and gave me a taste of cappuccino and a sandwich called the *medianoche*. He took us to Pinocchio's on Winthrop Street for our first pizza. He took us to Iruña on JFK Street and introduced us to *paella*, which reminded me a little bit of Indian *biryani*s and *pulao*s. He took us to a place called Genji, where we tasted our first sushi. The Architect tried to teach Ma and Baba the habit of drinking wine every evening. He gave them many lessons on how to drink red and white wines properly. Still, Ma and Baba never managed to become oenophiles and wine never became part of their evening ritual. There were so many rules, so many silent signals implicit in each mouthful. How an immigrant eats and drinks in America, I grasped quickly, was as important as how an immigrant speaks English. I redoubled my efforts to transform my palate as well as my accent.

By the autumn of 1983, I did successfully change my accent. Or so I believed. I cut the neckbands and waistbands off all my sweatshirts and wore them inside out. I pegged my pants. At the end of eighth grade, I was named the class valedictorian. My homeroom voted me the "most attractive" girl and the "most likely to succeed" in our yearbook. I was never invited to a dance in the school gym. The popular white girls did not include me in their slumber parties. The popular black girls never invited me to hang out after school. I stopped missing my old friends from Calcutta and formed a tight friendship with my Italian and Chinese friends.

I grew to enjoy the casseroles Ma was making, still guided by recipes from the backs of cans and boxes but with her own brave improvisations thrown in occasionally. When my friends asked me what Baba did for a living, I told little white lies or deftly changed the subject because I was embarrassed to say he was a salesman in a clothing store. Baba was clearly ashamed of his job and his shame infected me. To work in a clothing store, a place where a *darzi* might work, was considered beneath the social class to which we once belonged in India. Ma's job as a library assistant had a bit more genteel respectability. We had come from the Third to the First World, but our continued downward mobility of social class was not lost on any of us.

Nonetheless, there was one thing I refused to do despite all my early attempts at assimilation—I would not change my name. Many people asked me if I had a nickname, a shorter version of my given name. I did have another name. I still do. In fact, my natal family uses only that name and it is a very European-sounding name. Life in America might have been much easier for me in school, at university, and in the office if I had just told people my other name. I grow tired of having to spell my name out, letter by letter, while referring to other Western names. S as in Sam. H as in Harry. A as in Adam. R as in Robert. M as in Michael. I as in Isaac. L as in Larry. A as in Adam.

Sharmila is my legal name, the name meant for the outside world, while the other name, my *dak nam*, is for the home, for my natal family. Not even my in-laws or my husband calls me by my *dak nam*. I might give the barista a fake Christian name because I just want to know when my coffee is ready without adding more drama to the interaction. I might occasionally tell the pizza delivery guy my name is something else. Those are anonymous commercial transactions with someone I will likely never see again. Sharmila is my name for all other social encounters. I would give up cumin and coriander, my mother tongue, my old city, my old friends, those cows sleeping outside our door, Darwanji's spicy okra, Jamuna's tiger stories, the paper boats we floated on rainwater that collected in streams during the monsoon, the festivals that marked the seasons, green mangoes dipped in black salt, the joyful sound of ululation at a Bengali wedding, the feel of my grandmother's red-bordered white cotton sari, the happy sensation of bumping along sleepily on a three-tier Indian Railways train en route to see my grandparents, and even— one day in the future—my Indian citizenship. But my first name I would not give up no matter how many people in America complained it was too difficult to pronounce, too hard to spell.

Chapter Three

• • •

The Autobiography
of an Ex-Indian Woman

Going Native. Turning Turk. This is how we used to describe the actions of white people who wanted to look and act like people of darker complexions in exotic climes. In the eighteenth and nineteenth centuries, Going Native meant shedding European trousers and putting on a billowy *shalwar* or setting aside a top hat for a voluminous turban. Imagine British travelers such as Wilfred Thesiger, an Englishman who traversed the Empty Quarter of the Arabian Desert in the 1940s, accompanied by local tribes. Look at images of the Victorian adventurer Richard Burton, who supposedly went to Mecca disguised as a Muslim. Consider the sculpture of Edward Lane, a nineteenth-century English translator of the *Arabian Nights*, placed in a prominent corner of the National Portrait Gallery in

London. Wearing a turban and a loose robe, Lane sits cross-legged on a low platform—an archetypal image of the Oriental scholar lost in deep thought. A famous photo of T. E. Lawrence, better known as Lawrence of Arabia, shows him dressed in Arab clothing with a curved dagger hanging pertly against his waist. That is what Going Native looks like. Going Native means reclining on daybeds, sitting cross-legged on the floor, wearing turbans and kaftans, lining the eyes with kohl, smoking hookahs, eating spicy food, sharing bed and table with non-white women, exploring mosques and temples.

White Christians who converted to Islam in centuries past were said to have turned Turk. Turning Turk posed more of a threat to European identity, as it implied a change in creed. Turning Turk meant leaving Christendom forever and pledging fealty to a rival faith and a false prophet. Going Native, in contrast, could be a less permanent state of being. Thesiger left his tribal garb behind when he completed his travels in the Arabian Desert and returned to England. William Lane might sit permanently in a corner of London, frozen in his Egyptian robes, but in reality he too returned to English life and English clothes. White men who went native were almost always able to return to their white identity. Going Native is a type of drag. The pleasure of seeing a white man dressed as an Arab or an Indian springs from our awareness of his whiteness underneath the brownface, just as we can imagine male genitalia beneath female dress when we relish the performance of a drag queen. White Europeans who went native did not try to hide their whiteness completely. They flaunted their camouflage. They stood out precisely because they took such great pride in blending in. When I see these men in paintings, photographs, and lithographs today, I imagine them whispering, *Look at me. See my whiteness beneath these native clothes. See how good I am at being able to emulate the natives. See how my superior racial characteristics can never quite be muted by my exotic disguise.* When an Englishman went native in India in the eighteenth century he was disguising himself as someone who was not white. The power that Englishman derived from the disguise lay in the fact that he was *not quite* not white.

As Europeans began to have ambitions to grow their empires across the seas, the idea of Going Native and Turning Turk slowly appeared on the horizon. It was a scary threat and a delicious opportunity. It was also a liberating idea. What if instead of converting pagans, missionaries began to worship multilimbed gods? What if instead of civilizing people with darker complexions and flatter noses, Joseph Conrad's Kurtz became a savage himself?

In many cases, Going Native was a tactic for surviving in the competitive marketplace of colonial expansion. It was largely a male activity, though occasionally a white Christian woman might choose to wear exotic garb and enter a harem in order to uncover the secrets of the Orient. In India, during the British era, white men who went native often moved into the native section of town and lived with Indian wives and mistresses. These men wore Indian clothes, lived in homes with Indian-style decoration, ate Indian food using their fingers instead of silverware. They fathered mixed-race children. (My primary school teacher, Miss Solomon, was a descendant of their progeny.) Some of them began to worship new gods. They learned the local languages and sometimes spoke these languages with native fluency. Some even began to forget their English. To be more precise, their English became so peppered with the local argot that the language itself was in danger of becoming something else—*not quite* English.

In 1755, Samuel Johnson produced one of the most important modern dictionaries of the English language. The preface to the dictionary puts forth an intriguing argument for why the language was in need of standardization and codification. Proper English was in danger of Going Native in the distant corners of the British Empire as it mixed promiscuously in warehouses and ports with foreign tongues. "Commerce, however necessary, however lucrative," wrote Johnson, "as it depraves the manners, corrupts the language; they that have frequent intercourse with strangers, to whom they endeavor to accommodate themselves, must in time learn a mingled dialect, like the jargon which serves the traffickers on the Mediterranean and Indian coasts." Dr. Johnson's dictionary was intended to ensure that the

English language remained invulnerable to conquests and wanton migrations and did not assume too exotic a façade. Englishmen in the eastern colonies, meanwhile, draped yards of paisley shawls around their bodies.

Europeans who went native in India often lived two parallel lives. They had a brown family in the native section of town and a white family in the European section of town. They moved freely between the two. Their dual lives were an open secret and even considered an asset in their professional lives. Being able to go native—*and then being able to return to the white world unchanged*—could come in handy when there were vast native populations to rule. White women who married native men, lived in the native part of town, or gave birth to mixed-race children faced far greater difficulty in returning to the white world. They could not easily step out of a *ghagra*, tight-lace their corsets, and walk back to the European quarter. Their sexual intimacy with brown men would threaten European society in a wholly different way from the intimate relations between white men and brown women. In the eighteenth and nineteenth centuries, Going Native was largely *what men did*. And what men did was what counted as Going Native.

Could the native travel in the opposite direction? When you go native, where does the native go? If the British could speak my language, wear my clothes, eat my food, read my books, and occasionally even disguise themselves as me, then what was left for me to do? I do not know how my ancestors responded to the Europeans who went native in eighteenth-century India. But I do know that even now we Indians get a little overexcited when a white foreigner manages to say a few basic sentences in a local language. Their accent may be atrocious to the point of being unintelligible, but we praise them to the skies, pour them an extra cup of sweet *chai*, and immediately extend an invitation to the next family wedding. Such positive reinforcement is rarely on offer for non-white foreigners. Nigerians who might have picked up a few words of Kannada, or Chinese who can speak Bengali, do not get the sycophantic compliments reserved for whites in India.

When I was a young girl, an American woman who was working on her doctoral dissertation became acquainted with our family. From time to time, she would visit our Dover Lane flat unexpectedly. The Student used to spend many months in Indian villages and small towns for her fieldwork. When she came to Calcutta, she liked to go shopping, stock up on clothing and other necessities. Ma would take the Student to our favorite shops and help her choose saris she could wear during fieldwork. Ma also took her to our tailor so she could have blouses stitched. The Student was uncomfortable with the thin cotton voiles that were in fashion back then. She did not like the silhouette of her brassiere to be discernible beneath the semitransparent cotton. She also did not like the necks of her blouses to be cut too low, or the fabric to be fitted tightly around her chest. The

Student felt shy about baring her midriff when she wore a sari. She tied her sari in a way we city dwellers considered frumpy and rural—trying to hide her midriff by tying her inner petticoat too high, which resulted in exposed ankles.

Ma was bemused by the Student's fashion debacles. Yet, we were not dismissive of her. This was a white American woman who cared enough to learn about India, to wear a sari, to eat rice and fish curry with her fingers, to ask us for the Bengali names for things. We felt honored by her interest. Her high-water saris or frumpily cut blouses made of thick cotton were not considered a failure to assimilate, or a sign of her inferiority. Some years later, when we moved to the United States, we learned that the Student, having completed her doctoral degree, was now working at a prestigious East Coast museum. We never met her in America. I wonder what it would have been like if we did cross paths. Would the Student patiently take my mother to clothing stores and explain the latest styles? Would she be as forgiving if we made fashion mistakes or if we were unable to speak English clearly?

What is the opposite of Going Native? In colonial India, it meant becoming a *babu*. In the nineteenth century, the British referred to Indian men employed as clerks and administrative workers as *babu*s. The label always carried the sour aftertaste of derision. Over the course of time, *babu* became the name given to any middle-class Indian man with Western pretensions. *Babu*s were reviled by Europeans and Indians alike. They were brown Englishmen. They spoke English in a comical, florid way. They aped English manners and habits. The Indian orthodoxy hated them as race traitors. The English mocked them as wannabes. Being a *babu* is not really the opposite of Going Native, just as whiteface is never the opposite of blackface.

The opposite of Lawrence of Arabia is not Sharmila of America. When I decided to go native in America, to blend in with white dominant culture, I was following in the footsteps of a different group of people. Without knowing the word for it, I was passing. I am a seasonal Indian. My complexion is light enough for you to mistake me as Mexican, Greek, Arab, Iranian, Turkish, Spanish, or a Sephardic Jew. On the streets of America, I am often asked, *"¿Hablas español?"* When my skin darkens in the summer months, you might deduce that I am from the Indian subcontinent. If I wear a sari, line my eyes with kohl, or speak in the accent I once had, then you will see more easily that I am Indian. But I use camouflage frequently to lift the weight of visibility off my shoulders.

By the time I started high school, everyone had forgotten I was the foreign kid with a funny accent who had recently emigrated from Calcutta. After only two years of living in America, I was prepared to distance myself from my past. As countless American children before me had already discovered, the summer months between the end of middle school and the beginning of high school offered me the opportunity to reinvent myself. I was determined not to be a female version of a comical *babu*. I would not sound like Ben Kingsley in *Gandhi*. Nor would I look like those scrawny brown extras—the teeming masses of India waiting for the white man to give them independence.

● ● ●

Many years after my summer of passing had commenced, in a slim paperback novel that I had been assigned to read for a class, I came across this section:

"It is a difficult thing for a white man to learn what a colored man really thinks; because, generally, with the latter an additional and different light must be brought to bear on what he thinks; and his thoughts are often influenced by considerations so delicate and subtle that it would be impossible for him to confess or explain them to one of the opposite race. This gives to every colored man, in proportion to his intellectuality, a sort of dual personality; there is one phase of him which is disclosed only in the freemasonry of his own race. I have often watched with interest and sometimes with amazement even ignorant colored men under cover of broad grins and minstrel antics maintain this dualism in the presence of white men."[*]

These words were written by James Weldon Johnson in

---

[*] James Weldon Johnson, *The Autobiography of an Ex-Colored Man* (New York: Penguin Books, 1990), 14.

his classic novel of passing, *The Autobiography of an Ex-Colored Man*. Johnson's novel was first published anonymously in 1912. Scholars believe that he chose to keep his identity hidden in order to create buzz around the book's mysterious authorship. Was it a work of fiction or nonfiction? Was it a true revelation of a dark secret or a fanciful tale? Many assumed the novel to be a true autobiography written by an Ex-Colored Man. When first published, the book did not become a bestseller, win prizes, or receive many glowing reviews. It predated the Harlem Renaissance by almost a decade. In 1927, when the literary scene in New York had shifted considerably and works by black authors were fashionable in some circles, the publishing firm of Alfred A. Knopf reissued the novel. The Knopf edition carried James Weldon Johnson's name as the author of the book. By this time, Johnson was also the executive secretary of the NAACP, the first black man to hold this leadership position within the organization.

Johnson had written a novel, not a memoir. *The Autobiography of an Ex-Colored Man* is a deeply ironic work with a title that turns the theme of passing on its head. The Ex-Colored Man's race, far from being a secret, is flagrantly revealed in the title itself. The novel is both serious and flip—a tragic story told with comic wit. It holds up to the reader's gaze the limited story lines available for black male writers in early-twentieth-century America. The story itself, like its unnamed narrator, the Ex-Colored Man, has a dual personality. It teases us by pretending to reveal black secrets to white people. Is it written for a white audience only? Is it asking the reader to imagine what it is like to be a light-skinned black man? Or is it asking the reader—who might not be white—what it is like to be a white American who delights in peeking into black lives? In short, who is made to pass? The Ex-Colored Man or the reader? Who is made to traverse the dangerous fault lines of American civic belonging? The Ex-Colored Man or the reader?

If I were to go native in America, I had to figure out two things first: Which native was to be emulated? And who was my audience? No performance is complete without an audience. In order to research my role, I had to identify my audience. I had to understand which plotlines were legible to those who would read my body and my actions.

It was 1984. Ronald Reagan was elected to his second term after defeating Walter Mondale during the presidential election that fall. Though Ma and Baba were not eligible to vote, I eagerly watched my first American presidential elections on our black-and-white Sony television. Geraldine Ferraro was the first woman to be nominated for the position of vice president by a major political party. There was a lot of excitement over her. I understood that in America a woman could do many things that might have been frowned upon in India, but she could not become the head of state. Mrs. Indira Gandhi had been prime minister of India for much of my childhood years. As it came to pass, less than one week before Reagan defeated Mondale in 1984, Indira Gandhi was assassinated by her Sikh bodyguards in New Delhi.

Earlier that summer, I had been glued to the television each day, following the Olympic Games in Los Angeles. The USSR, East Germany, Iran, Libya, and a number of other countries had boycotted the games. In 1980, the Americans had boycotted the Moscow Olympics. I had read this in the Calcutta newspapers. A Russian scholar from Moscow who lived across the street from my grandparents had given me a commemorative pin from the Olympics. It was one of my most cherished possessions and came with me to Boston. A little golden pin with a cute brown bear—Misha—sporting the Olympic symbol as a belt. Anatoly, the neighbor who gave me the bear pin, also gave me a large pile of Soviet stamps for my stamp collection. I thought he was a very kind and generous man to give me such gifts. A few years later, removed from my native land, I was learning from television and school textbooks that communism was bad and the USSR was an enemy nation. America was where the good guys lived.

This was the backdrop against which the Ex-Indian Woman would be born.

• • •

At home when Ma and Baba spoke of Americans, pejoratively or admiringly, they really meant white Americans.

No one had to spell it out. Most Indians of my parents' generation, as well as some who are younger than them, continue to believe that "real Americans" are white Americans. All others are marked as deviations from the normative. American whites were not the only white people we knew. After all, the Portuguese, Dutch, French, and British all ruled various parts of India since the sixteenth century. Nonaligned India had strong political, economic, and cultural ties with the Soviet Union as well. We categorized all these white Europeans as *sahib* in Hindi, or *shaheb* in Bengali. A white man is a *sahib*. A white woman is a *memsahib*. Derived from an Arabic word for "owner" or "master," *sahib* did not have anything to do with race at first. It was a term of courtesy. In colonial India, however, *sahib* became a term used for white Europeans. *Gora*—literally "white"—is another word used by many Indians to designate white people. It is not a racial slur per se. Nonetheless, I know few Indians who would call a white person *gora* to his or her face, whereas in contemporary India, white men are addressed as *sahib* and white women as *memsahib* regularly. It is true that *sahib*, often shortened to *saab*, also continues on as a term of courtesy among Indians.

After three decades in this country, my parents continue to think that real Americans are white Americans. Everyone else is Not Quite. In those early years, when Ma and Baba spoke of American food, American homes, American customs, American habits, it was implicit that they were not speaking of those Americans who also happened to be black, or Chinese, or Hispanic, or Jewish. Ma and Baba did not quite appreciate the distinction between Catholics and Protestants and, consequently, were not able to tell how one group of white Christians might differ from another, let alone grasp which group was considered dominant. Could Asia, the continent from which we had emigrated, provide a way out? If our skin was too brown for us to pass as white, and if we did not wish to be seen as black, could we become Asian in America?

As a kid in Calcutta I thought I understood what the word "Asian" meant. I studied the geography of the continent. I knew about its physical features and political borders. My home state of West Bengal was ruled by the Communist Party of India. Consequently, as a young girl, I had studied the lives of Sun Yat-sen, Chiang Kai-shek, and Mao Zedong. I'd memorized the cash crops of the major Asian nations. I knew the length of the Yangtze River. I had learned how the silkworm makes silk. I had stared for hours at images of Mount Fuji on Honshu Island through the lenses of my View-Master. I had once proudly worn my red cherry-festooned Japanese socks even though I knew the nuns would be displeased if they caught me without my regulation navy blue socks. India was part of the continent of Asia. I was born in India. Therefore, I must be Asian.

Not Quite. In the United States, "Asian" was a code word for Chinese during the early 1980s. There was barely enough room for Koreans, Japanese, Vietnamese, or Filipinos to be included within this label. The Sinosphere loomed large in the mainstream imagination as the only way of understanding who was Asian. My Asianness was measured by my proximity to Chinese culture by the dominant white culture of the United States. It was a test of Asianness unlike any I had anticipated when I lived in an Asian city facing the Bay of Bengal. India had fought two wars with China during the 1960s. Sino-Indian border conflicts had hardened our attitudes toward the Chinese in India. Despite the prevailing anti-Chinese sentiments that cast a shadow on my parents' generation, who had lived through the Sino-Indian wars of the 1960s, older intellectuals such as my grandfather also reminded us of great Chinese scholars such as Faxian and Xuanzang who traveled to India during late antiquity. My grandfather even named Baba after a famous seventh-century Indian scholar at Nalanda who tutored the Chinese Buddhist monk Xuanzang. These stories were largely forgotten by most people in India when I was growing up. Yet, occasionally, a granddaughter remembered the stories recounted by her grandfather at dusk.

Chinese sojourners to India were not limited to Faxian or Xuanzang. The Calcutta Chinatown had a long history of Hakka immigration. Chinese women threaded Ma's eyebrows in south Calcutta beauty parlors. We devoured chicken sweet corn soup in restaurants owned by Calcutta's Chinese residents. My own upbringing in a Communist

Party–ruled state also gave me daily graphic reminders that "Chairman Mao is my Chairman" and "My name and your name is Vietnam." Those were the words written in Bengali on the walls of my Dover Lane neighborhood: *Mao amader chairman. Amar nam tomar nam vietnam.* Nonetheless, few Bengalis thought twice about using words such as "Chinky" to refer to the Chinese. Indian citizens from the northeastern part of the country—those areas bordering Tibet and Myanmar—are derisively referred to as Chinky on the streets of Delhi to this day. For the new Indian immigrant in the United States, being Asian suddenly meant becoming Chinky. The receiving country had its own terms and its own labels. To that we added the prejudices and the politics we had brought—along with those five suitcases and the green carry-on bag—from the sending country.

Despite being born and raised in an Asian country, becoming Asian in America was neither simple nor always desirable in the 1980s. The *CIA World Factbook*'s term for the Indian subcontinent—South Asia—had not yet gained currency in the American mainstream. Asia held little significance to most Americans, despite the two wars fought in Korea and Vietnam. Asian American celebrities or public figures were largely unknown to me in the early 1980s. Deng Xiaoping had barely started his experimentation with capitalism in Shenzhen, China's iconic Special Economic Zone. In the early 1980s, China and India were Asian nations known for their overpopulation, malnutrition, and low standard of living. With the exception of Japan, Asia was neither an economic powerhouse nor allowed a place at the high table of global politics. I had little incentive for claiming Asian American credentials.

My family is no different from the majority of Indian families who immigrated to the United States after 1965 in at least one aspect—our anti-black bias is strong. When I tried to pass as white, or silently accepted the badge of honorary whiteness, I was trying to proclaim to our neighbors that I was Not Black, that I was Not Hispanic. Every news story we saw on television, every innuendo Ma and Baba picked up around the workplace, every suspicious glance we spied in grocery stores, every gesture I clocked in the schoolyard taught us that blacks and Hispanics occupy the lower rungs of American racial hierarchy. As aspirational immigrants we aimed for a higher rung, desperate to impress the dominant culture with our work ethic, family values, and the antiquity of our culture. Emigration itself is risky enough. Having embraced one kind of risk, the immigrant needs to assess all other risks judiciously. The black figure, etched against the backdrop of white respectability and normalcy, stands for preposterous risks—economic, political, moral—from which the new immigrant, regardless of the exact shade of her skin, tries to inch away. Once you see the American racial hierarchy through the newly arrived migrant's eyes, you will understand why Toni Morrison once wrote that the road to becoming American is built on the backs of blacks. Many first-generation Indian immigrants in America boast of their low divorce rates and high household incomes; their old gods and their new-construction homes. Beneath these claims is a singular, fearful drumbeat refrain: *We are Not Black, we are Not Black, we are Not Black.*

Some older Indian immigrants worry that their child will marry outside caste or religion or linguistic group. Others worry that their child will marry a white person. But the greatest anxiety is that their child will marry someone black—the person being arrested for drug possession on countless television dramas; the person politicians tell us inhabit hellish inner cities and have nothing left to lose; the person who is shot by the police with frightening regularity. Immigrants from developing countries such as India are often afraid of the negative images associated with black America. These images remind them of the daily degradations they hoped to escape through immigration. The white-collar Indian who desires the symbols of American success—the right accent, Audis in the garage, an upscale suburban home, granite countertops, freezers with enough food to last an entire winter, a wine cellar, en suite bathrooms, backyards with barbecues, second homes, and even a foreign au pair—also wants to distance himself from the symbols of American failure. Sometimes it also means steering clear of one's fellow immigrant who has found less economic success in the promised land. Indian taxi drivers, gas station attendants, waiters, or hot dog vendors become less visible to the first-generation Indian immigrant who drives luxury cars, sends her children to private schools, and summers in Martha's Vineyard, just as the children of the Calcutta *basti* disappeared into the background when I held Ma's hand and walked down Gariahat Road.

For most of my life I have heard vulgarities such as Chinky, Negro, Red Indian, and even the N word casually used by many educated Indians without any sense of regret. Racist attacks against African students and tourists are a tragic reality witnessed regularly in major Indian cities nowadays. Anti-black bias is present among Indians in the home country as well as in the diaspora. In some cases, such as in the British West Indies, it was a result of social engineering by the European colonial masters as slaves were replaced by coolies on the sugar plantations. In the United States, the anti-black racism that many Indians bring with them from the subcontinent—a mixture of homegrown color bias and Made in Europe racism—is hardened by the prevailing myth of the model minority. These new immigrants, as well as some of their children, envision themselves as the embodiment of neoliberalism's promise. Judging their professional success to be a well-earned reward for hard work and merit, they remain blind to the historic disadvantages that prevent others from attaining similar success. To the white population the first-generation Indian immigrant wishes to say, "We are the model minority. The doctors who will heal you, the lawyers who will prosecute crime for you, the investment banker who will make you richer, the geek who will invent new technologies for your pleasure. We are the legal immigrants. Please don't confuse us with illegal ones. We're the good brown people. Please don't confuse us with the bad black ones."

Not Black. Not Quite Asian. My pale complexion—once of great value in the Indian matrimonial market—gave me an advantage that many other Indians do not have. Ma is darker than I am. My husband, a Punjabi Sikh, is darker than I am. So are my three children. I inherited my complexion from Baba. His accent is distinctly Indian. His name is unmistakably Bengali. Yet, Baba is often mistaken for white on American streets. As a teenager in America, I realized I could pass. And it felt good to disappear into whiteness, to become invisible.

· · ·

The customs of the country, as I learned them, were in actuality the customs of white people I wanted to emulate—those who bought expensive suits from the store where Baba worked, who I saw walking around confidently in Harvard Yard, employers who determined who got a job and who was sponsored for a visa, those who handed out my grades and my parents' paychecks, the people I saw reading the nightly news on television, the authorities who wielded power.

I began to construct an imaginary field guide for Going Native. Here is a small sampling from that old field guide, which I began in the 1980s. The invisible commentaries accumulated over subsequent decades as I tried to wear whiteface.

Upon Accepting a Gift

When given a gift always say thank you effusively. Hyperbole is useful—why be pleased when you can be ecstatic, elated, delighted, overjoyed, thrilled? Then open the gift and try it on, taste it, feel it, talk about it rapturously.

In Calcutta, when given a gift, we barely say a muted word of gratitude and promptly put the gift aside, unopened, feigning little interest in it. It is considered bad manners to do anything else.

On Thank-You Notes

Write thank-you notes for gifts received, dinner invitations, and all other acts of kindness. Use very good paper to write these notes and send promptly.

No one sends thank-you notes in India because the focus on goods received or meals eaten might make us seem greedy. In contrast, a well-crafted note of thanks is the mark of the socially well-groomed in America.

The Proper Response to Thank You

When someone says "Thank you," you must immediately say "You're welcome."

There is no Indian formula for this particular exchange. At most, we mumble "Mention not" in English. And we mean it. Do not mention it. Do not say thank you again. Do not send thank-you notes on fancy stationery.

The Blessed Sneeze

If someone sneezes, say "Bless you." Even if a stranger on a bus or a passerby on the street sneezes, you must immediately say this.

In India, millions of sneezes go unblessed daily.

The Indoor Voice

Do not speak loudly in restaurants. Use your indoor voice.

Indoor and outdoor voices are indistinguishable on the subcontinent, where domestic architecture often blurs the line between inside and outside. Everyone speaks as loudly as they want. The exception to this rule is that married women should always speak softly at home and in public. Loud, boisterous voices are best left behind for one's natal family. A soft-spoken daughter-in-law is a good daughter-in-law.

On Summoning Waiters

Always summon waiters as discreetly as possible.

In a restaurant, your power and status exist in inverse proportion to how loudly you have to speak to get attention from the servers. Powerful, wealthy white people only have to look up from their plate in order to summon a waiter. They make a quick motion with their hand, miming the act of writing, and the check appears. Words are for the powerless and second-class diners. In India, even the elite snap their fingers loudly and call out, "Bearerrrrr, bill!"

The Importance of Tipping

Always tip the waiter, the hairdresser, the pizza delivery man, the hotel chambermaid, and the taxi driver.

Few Indians consistently tipped waiters in the 1970s and there was no method of calculating a tip based on a percentage of the total cost of a meal at a restaurant. At most, people rounded off the bill, threw a few paisas on the table, and walked off. They did, however, believe in bribery and baksheesh. *A tip is for services already rendered. A bribe is to ensure future services.*

The Proper Use of Salt and Pepper

Never sprinkle salt excessively on your food. In a restaurant, pepper will be grated on your food by a waiter wielding something that looks like a small missile.

The Indian traditional thali, or plate, often comes with a tiny hillock of salt, a slice of lime, a green chili, and occasionally slices of raw onions. In India, no one will think you have a down-market palate if you liberally salt your food.

The Superiority of the Rare and the Dry

Bloodiest meat is best. Driest wine is best.

It required much work to put a piece of beef with little rivulets of blood trickling out of it into my mouth. I felt like I had summited Mount Everest when I actually came to enjoy the taste of an absurdly expensive piece of rare steak. The sort of meat we enjoyed in India was cooked until the flesh was falling off the bone. Southern barbecue is easier for an Indian immigrant's palate at first. Then one must work one's way up to carpaccio and steak tartare. From the cooked to the raw—this is how you climb the social ladder in America.

Only the socially inferior prefer their wines sweet in the West. Once upon a time, white sugar was a precious spice, reserved only for the aristocratic tables of Europe. Banquet tables laden with sugary desserts were an ostentatious display of power and wealth. Now, the consumption of white sugar, sweet drinks, and sweet wines is almost criminalized among the upper classes.

The Correct Use of Wineglasses

Red wine is to be drunk at room temperature in fat, round glasses. White wine is to be chilled and drunk from longish glasses. Red wine goes with red meat. White wine with fish and poultry. There are tricky exceptions. Proceed with caution.

During the 1980s, wine culture was largely unknown to most Indians. Middle-class men sometimes drank whiskey, rum, gin, or beer. Middle-class women did not drink openly, for to do so would make them look slutty. The upper and lower classes were free to do as they pleased. If a middle-class man thought a woman was "fast" enough to imbibe alcohol, he might offer her a drink with the mildly lecherous line, "Do you take?"

Silverware and Other Miscellanies at the Dinner Table

Do not eat with your hand in America.

In Calcutta, we eat Bengali food with our fingers. It is a delicate, high art when executed correctly. In America, I noticed some people even picked up their pizza slices or French fries gingerly, as if a fork and knife would be more appropriate. Forks on left. Knives on right. Spoons are for soups and desserts only. I sensed early on that the placement of silverware was not an innocent act. It can determine one's placement in the social hierarchy. Needless to say, possessing the right kind of tableware is also important. The newly arrived immigrant who finds success may buy all this. The cultural capital that accrues within the well-worn surfaces of heirloom china, crystal, or silverware remains painfully out of our grasp.

The paper napkin at the dinner table and the use of a spoon in place of a fork at mealtimes reveals the telltale heart of the newly arrived Indian on American shores.

The Unfortunate Smell of Curry

If you wish to assimilate into white American culture, do not smell of curry.

In India, no one speaks of the smell of "curry" because such a generic thing does not exist. Many different kinds of fragrances waft out of Indian kitchens. I knew which neighbor was simmering goat and which neighbor was frying cauliflower with nigella seeds. Our kitchens had open windows. In older homes, the kitchen was set apart from the rest of the house with an inner courtyard. No one checked their homes and clothes multiple times before guests arrived, anxious about the lingering odor of foreignness.

Odors and Other Unpleasantries

Use deodorant. Use mouthwash. Use dental floss.

When I was a young girl, these things were unheard of in average Calcutta households. Even hair conditioner was a new item in stores during the 1970s.

Queuing Up

Stand in a line politely and patiently. Do not attempt to cut a line. Maintain appropriate physical distance from others standing in line ahead of you and behind you.

American westerns told us the ideal American man was the outlaw or the cowboy. These men did not follow the niceties of Old World rules and were gun-toting, freedom-loving iconoclasts. American hippies who came to India relished breaking social rules. Yet, when it comes to standing in line, Americans are strict rule followers. Indians are line cutters. Indians often slyly inch their way up a line or find creative excuses for shoving others aside so they can get to the top of the line first. Indians also have a very different notion of what is considered acceptable personal space in comparison to Americans. Contact with other bodies in crowded buses, trains, and queues is a part of daily life in the subcontinent, and some even take comfort from this communal closeness. In America, by contrast, learning how to stand in line obediently, allowing enough space between the person ahead of you and the person behind you, is an important step in Going Native. Anything else is considered uncivil.

R.S.V.P.

Répondez s'il vous plaît.

    No one I knew in India asked for R.S.V.P.s in the 1970s. Even now few bother to R.S.V.P. Some will never show up to your dinner party, while others will arrive with six distant relatives, four friends, and two colleagues from the office. Luckily, Indian cuisine is marvelously flexible and a clever cook knows how to magically feed twenty people from a menu planned for ten.

The Gift That Has Been Registered

If invited to a wedding or a baby shower, always ask if there is a gift registry.

Americans will tell you exactly what they want you to buy them when they are getting married or having a baby. What you wish to give someone is of little consequence. What they want is more important. It is an efficient system of acquiring necessary, or even aspirational, objects. No one has to deal with the hassle of receiving fifteen glass pitchers of the same design. In India, while close relatives are expected to give saris or small pieces of gold jewelry, many guests bring cash to a wedding. Some hand over the cash to the official wedding gift collector, while others enjoy a good wedding banquet and depart with the cash safely tucked in their pocketbooks. Since gifts are only given after the birth of a baby, preregistering for baby gifts is still a rarity in middle-class India.

With each passing year my manual for Going Native continued to expand as new entries were added and older ones amended. I was author and exegete, maker and user, of my own field guide for the perplexed immigrant.

• • •

There were many other new rules that Ma, Baba, and I had to learn during our first few years here. Do not expectorate while walking on the street. Do not ask people how much their car cost. Do not ask how much they paid for their house. Do not ask whether they rent or own their house. Do not ask what their salary is. Do not tell anyone that they have gained weight or lost hair. Now that we owned a phone, we came to understand that we had to call ahead and make an appointment before visiting a friend or a relative.

Ma and Baba continued to read *Better Homes & Gardens* and *Reader's Digest*. Although we used to subscribe to the *Statesman* regularly back in Calcutta, we never subscribed to a single American newspaper after we immigrated. I do not know if it was because my parents felt less interested in the news here or if the unfailing presence of Peter Jennings and Dan Rather during our evening dinner hour made newspapers an unnecessary additional expense. As I grew older and started paying attention to the contents of certain high school classmates' living rooms, I noticed that their parents—the white, educated, professional ones— read publications that never crossed the threshold of our apartment: the *New York Times*, the *Wall Street Journal*, the *New Yorker*, the *Atlantic*, the *Economist*. My high school was located right next to the city's main public library. After school I headed to the reading room and thumbed through these publications, usually unable to follow the essays, or understand why a cartoon was funny.

When I saw the newspapers, magazines, and books that furnished the homes of successful, educated white people, I felt a certain kind of sadness for my parents. It was an emotion reminiscent of something I once read in

Bibhutibhushan Bandyopadhyay's *Aam Antir Bhepu*. This is the scene from the Bengali novel as I recall it: The young Apu—the unlikely namesake of the Kwik-E-Mart owner in Springfield—is eating a delicious meal at a wealthy villager's home in rural Bengal. At the end of the meal, he is served dessert—an unctuous semolina pudding, *mohonbhog*, studded with plump raisins and cashews and glistening with a generous helping of *ghee*, clarified butter. As he tastes the delicious *mohonbhog* he realizes it is far better than the version his mother makes at home. He feels a deep sadness rise within him as he continues to swallow each sweet mouthful. His family's poverty stands in ever greater contrast to his host's prosperity. But that is not the root cause of his heartache. Apu grieves for his mother because he imagines she does not know how a real *mohonbhog* must be prepared. As the wife of a poor Brahmin priest, Apu's mother's version is watery and innocent of expensive items such as raisins, cashews, or *ghee*. Middle-class, urban Bengalis of my generation who were raised on this classic novel will all remember how sad we felt when we reached this scene of rural impoverishment. We savored Apu's grief the way we enjoyed wiggling the loose baby teeth in our mouths. It was a sweet pain. I felt a similar melancholia when I saw a copy of the *Economist* in a classmate's living room. Ma and Baba had no idea why *New Yorker* cartoons were funny. They never read the op-eds in the *New York Times*. They never read book reviews in the *Economist*.

They were unfamiliar with this version of raisins, cashews, and *ghee*.

My appetite for self-improvement was the most American thing about me in those early teenage years as I was trying to go native. After devouring every issue of *Reader's Digest* and *Better Homes*, and after watching every TV show I could cram in without falling behind in school, I methodically read the entries in my most prized yard sale purchase—the *World Book Encyclopedia*. I even tried to teach myself a bit of French using that encyclopedia.

In seventh grade, the Peabody School introduced a second language to a select group of students. I am not sure how these students were chosen for French class. Perhaps they had the highest grades and were considered capable of taking on the additional burden of a second language. All the popular white kids were in French class. As a new student, I was not deemed eligible for French class. A few times a week, as many of the white students filed out for French class, I sat in a half-empty class with other kids who were not in French. We were told to use that period to review our work from other classes or start on homework. Some kids started homework, while others gossiped. Although I spoke English with a strong Bengali accent, I had no problem with following along in class or keeping up with my reading. Math and science classes did not challenge me in that first year because I had covered much of the material earlier in my Calcutta convent. I was hungry to learn more.

I was desperate to learn everything America had to offer. Those idle hours in class while others learned French in a separate room felt frustrating. I smarted with the humiliation I imagined was implicit in the school's decision to not allow me to learn French. We juggled three languages in three scripts—English, Bengali, and Hindi—in my Calcutta school. Surely, I could take a shot at French too. The following year, in eighth grade, it was determined that only those students who had already begun studying French in seventh grade would be allowed to go into second-year French. I was ineligible once more.

I could explain none of this to my parents. My grades in all the other classes were very good. My parents did not imagine there was any problem at school. Yet, I felt I was allowed to advance only so far in my new American school and then certain doors were being closed off so that I would always remain Not Quite. I learned how to count from one to one hundred in French from the encyclopedia, carefully trying to decipher the pronunciation of each number from its phonetic equivalent printed on the yellowing pages. *Un, deux, trois, quatre, cinq, six, sept, huit, neuf, dix.* Each evening I sat in with my encyclopedia and read about France and the French language. For no particular reason, I memorized the French motto of the British Order of the Garter—*Honi soit qui mal y pense.*

Why did French matter so much to me as a new American immigrant? The wealthier white kids in school all studied it. Some of them even spoke it at home. A few had traveled to France with their parents during summer vacations. French carried prestige. When the Architect took us to the nicer restaurants in Boston, the wine list had many French words on it. The Architect always translated the French words for us. A new bakery chain called Au Bon Pain had recently appeared in Boston. They served a delicious flaky pastry called a croissant. I wanted to understand what all these exotic words meant. I wanted to learn how to pronounce them like a native. I did not want America to be translated by the Architect forever. I wanted unfettered access.

Authentic French cookery was in vogue in America. Ma, Baba, and I lived a short distance away from Julia Child's home on Irving Street. We saw her cooking shows on WGBH, Boston's local public television channel. *Cassoulet, coq au vin, tarte tatin*—I devoured Julia's lessons, making note of every tidbit she dropped about her time in France along the way. Ma never cooked any of these dishes. As I got older I fibbed to my classmates and pretended we ate such food at dinner. I had seen enough of Julia's shows to imagine what that food must have tasted like. I would rather lunch off that imagined taste than bring leftover *roti* and *sabzi* to school. In high school I finally had my chance at enrolling in a French class. Our textbook, *Nos Amis*, taught us that French was spoken in Paris and Marseilles, as well as in Quebec, Martinique, and Tunis. We learned that French kids enjoyed Parisian croissants as well as Tunisian *briks*. We learned that French-speaking people shopped in *les marchés* as well as in *les souks*. Julia, however, continued to teach public television viewers French cookery as practiced in France.

White Americans were forever in pursuit of authentic tastes. French food in Provence. Italian food in Tuscany. The yearning to search for authenticity, for the origin of things, ran strong in the West. Wilfred Thesiger found the authentic spirit of Arabia in the desert tribes. He dismissed Arabs from polyglot trading ports or more cosmopolitan cities for not being as pure as the Bedu tribes whose ways apparently remained unchanged within the confines of the Rubʿ al-Khali. The Student who used to visit us in Calcutta and shopped for saris with Ma, similarly, would never consider us the proper subject of her research. Anthropologists such as the Student spent months with potters in Indian villages or tribals in remote hills. Forest-dwelling tribals and illiterate villagers were fitting subjects of American academic fieldwork. Middle-class, anglicized, city dwellers—Indians like Ma, Baba, and me—were not authentic enough. The real India was to be found in mud-hut villages and tropical jungles.

The desire to conquer the wilderness stretched from the early European colonists in the New World to Captain James Tiberius Kirk. Television taught me that the final frontier beckoned even in the future. White Americans

wanted to boldly go where no man has gone before. I identified with the crew of the USS *Enterprise* because I too
found myself far from home, exploring strange new worlds,
seeking out new life and new civilizations.

• • •

One summer, early in high school, I developed a sudden
obsession for no-bake Jell-O desserts. Every afternoon,
when my parents were at work, I created pastel-colored
delicacies based on recipes I found in advertisements for
Cool Whip and Jell-O. A dreamy pale pink strawberry
mousse. A light green key lime pie. Quivering multicolored
parfaits. Each evening, when my parents returned home
from work, I liked to surprise them with my new American
creations. One afternoon, while I was busy making another
no-bake mousse or pie, Ma came home during her lunch
hour with a colleague from work. He was a tall, lanky,
white man with wispy brown hair. Ma had told me about
him earlier. He drank wheatgrass juice, ate only organic,
vegetarian food, and avoided white sugar. He came home
with Ma to learn how to make *paneer*.

I stood in a corner of our kitchen—the same one where
we found a white lace curtain and a half-empty container
of Brigham's strawberry ice cream—and watched Ma bring
a pot of milk to boil. She carefully cut some limes into
halves. When the milk was bubbling, she reduced the heat,
then squeezed the lime juice into the pot. The milk curdled

and the entire kitchen was filled with the aroma of citrus and dairy. Then Ma poured the curdled milk into another pot, straining the liquid through a square of thin muslin. The solids collected in the muslin, and Ma, with an experienced flick of her wrist, gathered up the cloth into a small pouch, squeezing the contents. The remaining liquid squirted into the pot. Ma weighed the muslin pouch down with a heavy plate. The brown-haired man was observing her every move with great attention, asking detailed questions. In Bengali we called this type of cottage cheese *chhana*. Since Ma's colleague only knew it from Indian restaurants, he called it *paneer*.

After a few minutes had passed, Ma unwrapped the muslin and a small disk of fresh white *paneer* was revealed from the inner folds of the cloth. She cut him a piece. He ate it deliberately, relishing each bite. The look on his face puzzled us. Today, I can decipher that look. Richard Burton must have had it when sharing a meal with the faithful in Mecca. Wilfred Thesiger too, when breaking bread with the Bedu in the Rubʿ al-Khali. We wear it when we take a wrong turn in a foreign city and find ourselves in a small alley with a little nameless café that has only four tables. We have it when we sit down at one of those four tables, the others being occupied by natives who speak in a language we do not understand, and point to whatever the others are eating. It is the look we have when we recall this meal in a nameless café in a foreign city and remark how very good it was to discover it before the tourists destroyed it.

Ma wrapped up the remaining *paneer* and handed it to her colleague to take home. For months afterward we continued to laugh at the absurdity of that afternoon. In Calcutta, making *paneer* was as straightforward for Ma as making toast. In Cambridge, a white man had followed her home, sat in our kitchen, and observed her preparing it with the same gaze of admiration one sees around a circus performer. Ma knew it was all a bit of theater. The role was scripted by someone else, the scene was directed by someone else, and the audience was white. We knew that this theater was a trap.

If Ma cooked as she did in Calcutta every day, if she made *paneer* every day, then we would remain authentic. That kind of authenticity is mute and keeps you imprisoned in a small kitchen in an attic apartment. It requires the seal of approval from the brown-haired white man. He speaks as our proxy. If we cling to that authenticity for too long, others would come to accuse us of not assimilating. On the other hand, if we cooked from recipes found on a Campbell's can and on the back of a Bisquick box, then we would no longer be the real deal. We would be mongrels, hybrids, wannabes, Not Quites. As immigrants we were in a rush to fit in with the new country to the best of our ability. We did not wish to stand out, call attention to ourselves. The natives of the new country, especially the white ones, were rushing all over the world meanwhile, searching for the most authentic sashimi, for the truest sole meunière, for the most virginal of olive oils. Which natives were we supposed to emulate? Anti-black bias compelled us to differentiate ourselves from Americans of darker hues. Anti-Chinese bias made us hesitate to enter the big tent of Asian America. And in our attempt to go native, we turned a blind eye to other natives—the other Indians—who had been brutally pushed aside as part of the conquest of the wilderness.

Once upon a time, a type of American story, written usually by white settlers, circulated widely in the colonies. It was called the captivity narrative—white European accounts of being held captive by the natives of the New World, the Indians. The most well-known of all American captivity narratives, *A Narrative of the Captivity and Restoration of Mrs. Mary Rowlandson*, was printed in 1682 by Samuel Green in Cambridge, Massachusetts, exactly three hundred years before Ma, Baba, and I arrived in the same city from India. Mary, as it happens, was a first-generation immigrant herself, landing in Salem from England sometime around her thirteenth year. The American captivity narrative is an inversion of the slave narrative. The author, usually a white Christian captured by Native Americans, offers a tell-all story of redemption and survival behind enemy lines. Slave narratives are also stories of captivity, with the important distinction that the captors themselves are Christians. The slave narrative works by appealing to the (white) audience's sympathy for a person who can adopt superior Christian morals, even if her skin retains a darker hue. The captivity narrative works by appealing to the (white) audience's sympathy for a person who bravely retains her superior Christian morals, despite being forced to live in a society of savages with darker skin. For one group, slavery is the smithy of the soul where the uncreated conscience of a race is forged. For another group, captivity is the smithy of the soul where the preexisting conscience of a race is tested.

Going Native and becoming an Ex-Indian Woman in my quest for acquiring social privilege led me to scavenge for all manner of fragments so I could piece together what transpired in America during those intervening three centuries that separated the two immigrant girls—Mary and myself.

. . .

Privilege is a peculiar possession. To those who possess it, privilege is weightless, tasteless, odorless, soundless, and colorless. Those who have the least access to it are painfully aware of its mass, density, taste, odor, texture, sound, and color. When I first came to the United States and suddenly became a minority, I felt the weight of a peculiar kind of visibility. Once I had worn the mantle of privilege lightly on my shoulders. Now I could not shake my awareness of the constant expenditure of energy required in everyday life when social privilege is taken away. Frantz Fanon, a twentieth-century black intellectual famous for his critique of colonialism, wrote that one of the long-lasting legacies of European empires was third-person consciousness. In his native Martinique, as well as in Europe and North Africa, Fanon argued, the black man always saw himself through the eyes of the white man. The black man always perceives himself in the third person. "Look, a Negro!" That is what a white child says to his mother while pointing to Fanon. "Look, a Negro!" That is what Fanon and countless other black people, enslaved and colonized, say to themselves. They become visible to themselves only as a figure one sees in a distorted mirror. They cannot look out and see the world without always looking at themselves first as that reflection in the mirror.

To always think of oneself in the third person—*she, he, it, they*—is to lose the first person—*I, me, we, us*. This is the condition of being hypervisible. The hoodie, the beard, the turban, the headscarf, the burka, the burkini, and the bindi all set off alarms when we are scanned by the laser beams of surveillance. In the worst of circumstances, hypervisibility makes neutral physical markers—the color of our skin, the shape of our eyes, how we wear our hair, how we dress—glow with radioactivity. In the best of circumstances, hypervisibility sets the minority apart from the majority, the marginal apart from the normative, just enough so that bridging the gap incurs further expenditure of energy. Some people tire of these constant expenditures. They tire of the little glosses, the translations, the analogies, the spelling and pronunciation guides required for unusual names, the explanations that must accompany certain kinds of dress or hair, the nonverbal compensatory assurances that must be provided when a foreign sentence slips out. Hypervisibility is not celebrity or fame. The hypervisible person of color, following Fanon's logic, is nothing like a movie star with millions of followers on social media. Imagine instead a world in which you have no words of your own to understand yourself. Imagine instead a world in which every word and every concept you would apply to yourself has been created by people who see you as inferior, as threatening, as other. Third-person consciousness makes me see myself *only* as others see me. I become foreign to myself.

I wanted none of it. I wanted to *see* and not bear the burden of *being seen* at all times. I did not want to stand out, marked as different. I wanted a little bit of the life I once had in Calcutta, where no one needed me to spell my name or ask me where I really came from. I wanted to blend in. The great current of American assimilationist ideals was flowing in the same direction. Immigrants are supposed to abandon themselves to the energetic whirl of American culture. Those who do not embrace their host country, who do not learn the language, adopt the values, or fly the flag, were considered as problematic thirty years ago as they are today. Failure to assimilate can lead to accusations of ingratitude, incompetence, or, worse, infidelity to the host nation. I learned to modulate my voice. I checked my clothes so that I did not leave the house smelling of cardamom, cloves, cumin, garlic, or ginger. I learned what to drink, eat, wear, and read as part of my DIY whiteface.

At university I learned more tricks for manipulating language. Tricks that I could have never imagined when the best I could do with English was to identify a banana and name its color. I learned how to turn a noun into a verb. How to throw in a French phrase here. How to add a German word there. How to embellish a sentence with some Latin. Never would I add any Bengali or Hindi words to my English. Such things are celebrated within the fictional universe of Booker Prize–winning novels, but not in an American office or classroom. In the comforting privacy of countless student apartments, coffeehouses, and bars of New Haven I spoke in Hindi and Bengali to fellow Yalies who came from the same part of the world as me. To the very few black students I knew in my PhD program I could speak freely about our shared but distinct conditions of Not Whiteness. I asked these friends why my cheeks hurt from smiling. Everywhere else I tried to fade into the dominant culture of the campus. I wore whiteface.

Did I become white? Was I trying to be white? That was neither possible nor desired. I was an Ex-Indian Woman who acted white. I was never admitted into the freemasonry of the white race.

• • •

Acting white in certain ways, and achieving the financial success associated with white professionals, meets with resounding approval in Indian immigrant homes. One can go only so far, however, and then it is time to apply the brakes. Indians draw a distinction between light-skinned people like me and actual white people. An Indian woman whose complexion is pale enough to make her look like a "foreigner" back in the home country might be highly prized by grandmothers looking to arrange a marriage. Nevertheless, she must only *look like* a white foreigner, not actually *be* one. Religion, caste, ethnolinguistic groups still carry significant weight in the subcontinent, where many families look unfavorably upon interracial unions.

I was an Ex-Indian Woman who was supposed to act white without actually becoming white. Perversely, this arrangement suited America's dominant culture as well. After all, imitation is the best form of flattery. By acting white, I was flattering the dominant culture. And by remaining Not Quite White I posed no threat to white elites. I would forever be the light-skinned foreigner at the table. The one who appreciates all the good things about Western civilization—Doric columns, Shakespeare, democracy, good wine, high-quality cheese, essays in the *New York Review of Books.* And I would also remain a member of a race who did not invent any of these things.

After so many decades, I had landed right back where Thomas Babington Macaulay's plan started in 1835. The goal of English-medium education in India, Lord Macaulay had said, should be to create a class of Indians who would be interpreters between whites and natives. This creature would have English tastes and values, but Indian blood. Values and tastes, our colonial masters once believed, were changeable. Superior, white, Western tastes could be taught to inferior races. Blood, however, was unchangeable. In truth, neither bloodlines nor culture could be kept pure. Macaulay chose to ignore those people who were both English and Indian by blood. Instead, he focused on a different sort of mixing that would produce the interpreter class. The children of white men who went native—Miss Solomon, Merle Oberon, and others like them—were not the intended outcome of colonial rule. My ability to appreciate the proportions of Greek architecture, to relish the boldness of a Joyce novel, to think according to rules fixed in a continent far from my place of birth—these were all intended outcomes. It would not be too much of a stretch to say that the Ex-Indian Woman was all the British Empire intended. The seeds were planted centuries ago. The flowering occurred in the New World.

When I was in New Haven, whiteface meant distancing

myself from my Indianness while never being fully untethered from it. Whiteface meant being Not Quite White, Not Quite Indian, Not Quite Black, Not Quite Asian. It pleased the Indian immigrants with aspirations of making it and leaving behind a world that stank of curry. It pleased middle-class whites who glimpsed in my newfound tastes and habits a buttressing of their many convictions: Ben Jonson got it right when he said Shakespeare was for all time. John Winthrop could not have said it better when he preached that we are as a City upon a Hill and the eyes of all people are upon us. Manifest Destiny is the patrimony of all U.S. citizens.

I was happy to please so many different kinds of people. Still, my cheeks hurt from smiling.

· · ·

My adventures in Going Native did not end there. There were further removes to be completed. The brown-haired man who came to watch Ma squeeze lime juice into boiling milk had already shown us the path. Ma was not the only one who had something to teach that afternoon when she made *paneer*. The brown-haired man had something to teach us as well. He taught us that loving lots of other exotic cultures is part of advanced DIY whiteface curriculum. In the beginner stage, people like me only know how to navigate between two poles—white and non-white. Understanding that there are diversities within each of these categories, and that they are available for us to breezily celebrate, consume, own, and master, is the real key to acting as a privileged white American.

Mastering the English language, learning how to hold the fork with my left hand and the knife with my right hand, or drinking red wine from the correct glass was the first remove. If I truly wanted to act like the white customer who purchased suits from the store in Harvard Square where Baba worked during the 1980s, I had to learn how to hold chopsticks properly. What good is my knowledge of wines if I do not know how to order sake during a business dinner in a high-end Japanese restaurant in New York? What good is the ability to correctly identify the salad fork if I fumble with chopsticks during an important client meeting in London's Hakkasan? Catching the allusion to Milton's *Paradise Lost* during a graduate school reception in New Haven might earn me a faint nod of approval from a professor. If I could respond with a carelessly tossed-off line from the great Portuguese epic *The Lusiads*, then I would make an even more favorable impression on the same faculty member.

On Ivy League campuses, I encountered certain whites who held steadfastly to the idea that the entire world was waiting to be read, eaten, seen, photographed, tagged, analyzed, and *known* by them. Nothing in their lives contradicted this conviction. Often they identified as political liberals, forward-looking, open-minded, tolerant people.

They broke publicly with those whites who had once believed that the Orient was inscrutable and Africa was a dark continent. They studied languages, traveled extensively, took pride in their adventurous palates, and decorated their homes with souvenirs scoured from bazaars and souks and *tiendas* spotted in the farthest corners of the world. Their bookshelves sagged under the weight of books printed in many languages, bearing the colophons of publishers from all over the world. No culture or people was unknowable to these people. They were experts on all manner of subjects, from the plight of the Rohingya refugees in Myanmar to the role of Kurds in Turkish national politics. They could read the inscriptions found on Shang dynasty oracle bones as easily as they could explain the Brazilian political economy. They could speak knowledgeably about ancient Javanese literature and the poetry of Pablo Neruda. The newly arrived immigrant, meanwhile, could only move between two places—sending country and receiving country, my alpha and my omega. In graduate school, none of what I knew during the first twelve years of my life in Calcutta counted as knowledge. Trying to get ahead by increasing my knowledge of the West was like trying to earn a living by gambling in a casino. The house always won.

Slyly, I shifted my focus from the West to the Rest: I began to learn about Africa, South America, the Caribbean, West and East Asia. I enrolled in classes where I read books written by men and women from Cuba, Barbados, Guyana,

Martinique, Kenya, Nigeria, Zimbabwe, and Egypt. I studied the art, architecture, cinema, history, politics, and languages of Ottoman Turkey, French Africa, and the British Caribbean. In these classes the students could be divided into two categories: One group could trace some part of their ancestry to the region and the other group was white. Minorities were free to pursue their "heritage"—a prefab house designed according to the prevailing wisdom of the dominant culture. Minorities were also free to study the West. Whites, on the other hand, could study anything they wished. The confusion always arose when one deviated from the color-coded pathways designed for us. The Indian woman who enrolled in a Francophone Caribbean literature seminar, or the Chinese man who wanted to learn Egyptian Arabic, or the Jamaican woman who set out to specialize in ancient Chinese history—we confused the system. In liberal arts schools, a certain amount of dilettantish range was encouraged. When it came time to hunker down and choose a major, to stake out one's future professional turf, the old formula still held true—whites could roam freely all over the world, while non-whites had limited access. Non-whites could focus on the West and try to make their mark in it (and many did so exceedingly well) or they could inhabit those parts of the world where the natives most resembled them in race, religion, or language.

The last remove of DIY whiteface is what Western corporate jargon infamously terms "opening the kimono."

When you open the kimono you reveal a secret in order to gain the trust of the other party. It is a high art and should not be attempted by the novice. This was the postscript to my field guide to Going Native. You open the kimono in whiteface performance by subtly revealing something exotic about yourself. A bit of non-whiteness peeks out like the beautiful silk lining of a bespoke suit, and your heretofore hidden past becomes a commodity that can be traded to climb the social ladder. To this end, I started serving *dal* in teacups as a first course during dinner parties; I cut long scarves out of Ma's old silk saris and twisted the soft textile around my neck; I framed a poster of an old Bollywood film and hung it up in a room carefully decorated with midcentury modern furniture; I left a book on Indian art published by a famous American museum on my coffee table when visitors stopped by. Everything was meant to look effortless. Everything was controlled and measured so as to offer only the subtlest heat of Indian spice. I wanted to appear worldly and sophisticated without teetering into Fresh Off the Boat territory. It was as delicate an act as putting on eyeliner before a party. Too much looks downmarket and too little makes no impact at all. Revealing a bit of strategic brownness during whiteface performance is no different.

In *The Autobiography of an Ex-Colored Man*, James Weldon Johnson wrote that each black man possesses "in proportion to his intellectuality, a sort of dual personality . . .

even ignorant colored men under cover of broad grins and minstrel antics maintain this dualism in the presence of white men." When I first read of this dualism, I imagined it to be a type of split personality. I thought that black men revealed their authentic selves to other black men, while presenting a false face with broad grins to white men. As I reread that passage over the years I saw that Johnson was pointing to a far more complex sort of dualism. For some, the dualism could be a prison house of doubleness, an inner sundering of an original whole. For others, the dualism could be the opposite of a prison house. It could be the escape tunnel that allowed one to *go native* and *play the native* at the same time.

I opened the kimono. I wore a sari. To my dismay, those nine beautiful yards of handloom cotton that Ma once wore every day in Calcutta suddenly felt like a Halloween costume on my body. I had commodified my own past and offered it up for the delectation of others. I was an Ex-Indian Woman who had accidentally gone native in the old colonial style. I was reclining on daybeds, sitting cross-legged on the floor, lining my eyes with kohl, and smoking hookahs. I was a brown woman mimicking a white man pretending to be a brown man.

Chapter Four

• • •

Heart of Not Whiteness

As a new immigrant I nursed high ambitions. Fresh off the boat, FOB, I refused to be. American-born confused Desi, ABCD, I could never be because I was not American born. I squirmed at the mediocrity associated with those we Indians derisively called "coconuts"—brown on the outside, white on the inside—with suburban split-level homes, two-car garages, finished basements with wet bars, Indian channels on cable, and Americanized names in the office. I desired the life of upper-class whites, the kind who had summer homes in Nantucket and their great-grandmother's Spode china in the pantry. I wanted to be the sort of woman who frowned upon tourists and called herself a traveler. The kind of person who collected textiles, ornaments, spices, and decorative objects from travels to dustier, hotter, and poorer places in the world. I admired the confidence with which such people mispronounced foreign words and proudly displayed their cosmopolitan credentials by watching art-house foreign films.

My dream of living the life of an affluent white American was not a consequence of forgetting India. Until I graduated from college, I spent a couple of months in India nearly every other year. They were hot summer months that melted into the torrential monsoon season. I spent many nights sleeping with the entire family on my uncle's Delhi rooftop. I snuck away with my Lucknow cousins to eat *chaat* in Hazratganj and *kulfi* in Aminabad. I watched the rain clouds darken the skies of Goa. I whispered and giggled late into the night with my cousin in Santiniketan. My uncle and I traveled by train from Delhi to Bombay, feverishly repeating old stories of boring weddings and lively funerals, reliving the thrill of domestic scandals that tighten the bonds of large families with each retelling. One grandmother massaged Pond's cold cream on my face each night when I visited her in Allahabad. Another grandmother complained that all her servants were thieves. India was changing rapidly during those first two decades of economic liberalization. Cars, color televisions, VCRs, telephones, fast-food shops, discotheques, and malls were becoming more common in the big cities. Moviegoers swooned over new heartthrobs. I watched *Mr. India* and *Maine Pyar Kiya* multiple times in the cinema halls. I purchased large piles of

Filmfare and *Stardust* magazines each time I returned to India in order to stay abreast of the latest gossip about Salman Khan. I wished I could dance like Sridevi and Madhuri Dixit. I longed for Dimple Kapadia's lustrous mane. I dreamed of Shahrukh Khan waiting for me on the Swiss Alps, a sweater draped on his shoulders, his mullet blowing in the breeze, his arms wide open. And then, as soon as my plane touched down at Logan Airport, I stowed away that part of me—the rooftop-sleeping, *chaat*-eating, Salman-fangirl part—in the back room of my mind.

In Boston, I left my Bengali locked up at home, spoke Hindi only in private with a few select friends, and was careful never to mispronounce English words. If I wore a sari to attend a Durga *puja* celebration in the basement of a suburban church with my mother, I made sure none of my American friends saw me. I avoided watching movies about India, such as *Salaam Bombay!*, *Slumdog Millionaire*, or *The Lunchbox*, with white Americans. The sincere conversations over a cappuccino or a glass of wine that inevitably followed such movies were dreadful for me. I was expected to discuss human rights, the poverty of slums, the plight of untouchables, child marriage, and widow burning. I had to play the native informant, as well as the assimilated immigrant. My presence completed the cosmopolitan experience for my white friends and reassured them of their own open-mindedness, generosity of spirit, liberal politics, and cultural superiority. And my cheeks hurt from smiling through it all.

In college, I would sooner watch the newest summer blockbuster with my white friends than go for a marathon screening of Satyajit Ray or Ritwik Ghatak films. I would sooner discuss Nella Larsen's *Passing* than Rabindranath Tagore's *Gora*. I would sooner write an essay on Odysseus's return to Ithaca than Ram's return to Ayodhya. I lived in multiple worlds. I did not want my Indian world to touch my American one.

Predictably, I was also drawn to those very places where my two lives collided. As an undergraduate, I enrolled in classes that focused on the Indian subcontinent. I gingerly ventured into the South Asian students' association on campus, knowing that I would never be fully at home with second- or third-generation diaspora kids or be able to share the views of international students who had recently arrived on campus. I participated in our college's annual South Asian variety program. In fact, back in 1989, I was one of the founding members of the show. During its first few years it was very much a small affair—attended only by *desi* students and their parents. Twenty-five years ago, *bhangra*, *garba*, and Bollywood dance were fairly marginal on American campuses. Few white students were interested in watching those shows, let alone gyrating along with us.

We were a few years behind our British counterparts in bringing *desi* rhythms and style to mainstream American pop culture and to the dance music scene. By the nineties, I was listening to British musicians, such as Talvin Singh, who were crafting the Asian Underground sound across the Atlantic. "Flight IC408" and "Chittagong Chill" by State of Bengal and Apache Indian's "Chok There" promised something cooler, more confident, more political, and more fun than anything an American life in whiteface had to offer. A quarter of a decade ago, if you were a young college student looking for this sort of music, you had to venture to the Asian clubs and South Asian student parties on American campuses. Those were the places where you might hear *bhangra* crossed with reggae, Baul melodies mixed with electronic music, or Indian classical instruments incorporated into drum and bass tracks. To not be part of the mainstream dance music scene was fine by me.

By the time I was a senior in college, our little student variety program had grown to attract bigger crowds. We performed in a real auditorium and the people who came to watch us were not all *desi*. The growing popularity of our show gave rise to mixed emotions. It felt good to receive a small amount of mainstream attention. Yet, a part of me also felt uncomfortable with our growing audience. It was one thing to perform a so-called classical dance in front of white students. I danced *kathak* and some of my classmates performed *bharatanatyam* pieces. Even if the people in the audience did not quite understand the stories enclosed within each gesture or glance, or the distinct mood of each piece, the dances were perceived to be dignified. The presence of a *tabla* or a *sitar* onstage lent a touch of respectability to the entire performance. It was something else entirely to wear sparkly synthetic saris, with stacks of glass bangles on each wrist, and throw myself into the delirious beats of a *garba* or to gyrate and whoop to loud *bhangra* beats. This was the popular culture of the place I had left behind. It was about having fun, and not about showing white America that we were the proud heirs of an ancient civilization. Amitabh Bachchan and Rekha flirted to the tune of *rang barse*. Sridevi sang naughtily about the *nau nau churiyan* on her wrists. Madhuri provocatively asked us to guess what was hidden behind her *choli*. This wasn't the India of art-house films, or the India admired by the brown-haired man who learned how to make *paneer*, or the India of the Student who wrote about potters in villages and wore high-water saris. It was not the India of Attenborough's *Gandhi*. This was the India I relished; the movies I liked to watch at home with my parents when we missed our old neighborhood; the songs I enjoyed in private; the dance moves, the *jhatka*s and *thumka*s, I tried out in front of the bathroom mirror when no one was watching. I was not ready to share this India with America.

My carefully partitioned worlds brushed even closer together when I took a job as a freelance interpreter. Throughout my undergraduate years, I always held down a variety of work-study jobs on campus. Occasionally, I needed to look outside the college for opportunities to make a little extra income so I could pay for textbooks, late-night snacks, and discounted clothes from Filene's Basement. One day I saw a flyer advertising a job for freelance translators and interpreters. One of the languages the flyer listed was Bengali. I'd never imagined my mother tongue could lead me to a job in Boston. A few weeks after I sent in my resume, I learned that I was selected for the position.

Almost all of my freelance assignments involved deportation cases. My experience as an interpreter could be summarized as this: I stood in Boston courts and told Bangladeshi immigrants that they were to be deported. The court officials instructed me to repeat what was being said by each party during the proceedings and not add any of my own opinions. I was not to engage in side discussions with the defendants. I listened to what the lawyers and judges said in English and repeated it to the Bangladeshi men as accurately and concisely as I could. The men usually spoke to me in rural dialects of Bengali. Our shared mother tongue made the disparity of our circumstances amply clear.

I was a Hindu Bengali from Calcutta who spoke with the accent of an upper-middle-class educated woman. I spoke what was "standard Bengali" in Calcutta—the way radio broadcasters who read the Bengali news during the 1970s spoke. In the courtroom, I was dressed in American clothes, speaking American English that had been further honed at an Ivy League campus. I was light skinned enough to be mistaken for white. The defendants were Muslim Bangladeshis, often from the rural areas of their country. They spoke Bengali with a "regional" accent—the way someone from a village with little access to formal education in any language speaks. They were sometimes dressed in orange. They were invariably much darker in color than me. No one would mistake them for white in America. If I was the model minority, the young immigrant who had made it, they were the unwanted minority, the immigrants who caused trouble. They were the problem—the reason why immigration is bad for America. I was the solution—the reason why immigration is good for America.

Did we follow the court's instructions? Not always. The men who were unable to speak English often slipped in some questions for my ears only. *What are they saying, sister? What is going on? Is there any way you can help me? What should I say? Please tell me what to say and I will say it, sister.* My answers were brief, spoken almost coldly. I had to slip them in while I was relaying the official utterances of the judges and lawyers. If I spoke for too long, or if I showed any emotions, then the court would know I was not following the rules. *Don't ask me these questions, brother. I am not supposed to speak to you directly. I don't know how to help you. I am sorry. I am sorry. Please ask your lawyer to help you. I cannot answer your questions. I am sorry, brother.*

I recall a particular deportation case especially well. When the judge finally handed down the verdict, I had to tell two men—men who spoke the same language I spoke, who came from the same part of the world where my grandparents had been born, who knew how to eat fish curry and rice with their fingers as I did, how ripe jackfruits smell in the hottest months of summer and how green guavas taste with a little sprinkling of black salt, how day can turn into night within minutes when a *kal boishakhi* storm descends upon Bengal—they were to be deported. The truth is I do not know the exact Bengali equivalent for "deportation." I had no call to learn that word in Calcutta. I turned to the defendants and spoke in the politest Bengali I could muster, as if we were conversing about poetry over a cup of Darjeeling tea: *Brothers, these gentlemen are requesting you to please take your leave from here.* Their expressions clearly betrayed a rudimentary grasp of English. They had guessed the verdict even before I started addressing them in Bengali. Yet, I felt the need to use our mother tongue with great care and eloquence. The English of the courtroom was bureaucratic, lacking in beauty and heart. Their English told the truth. But my Bengali told it slant. A few weeks later, I received a small check in the mail as payment for my work. I never took a freelance job with that company again. It was time for me to find other ways of augmenting my student income.

Bangladeshi migrants are a common sight in the gated

communities that have sprung up in Delhi suburbs such as Gurgaon and Noida. Many of these migrants work as maids in the homes of middle-class Indians, including Bengalis. Some of these Bangladeshis are Hindus. Bangladesh, a Muslim-majority nation, continues to be home to a sizable Hindu-minority population. Nonetheless, the Hindu Bengalis of India still see these migrants, who speak their language and worship their gods, as inferior. They are illegal immigrants. They do not have the same rights as Indian citizens. They are poor. They are the underclass. They live in slums. They exist to keep the floors of high-rise apartments sparkling and wash the newly affluent class's dirty dishes. Muslim Bangladeshis are treated with even greater suspicion. They are the familiar stranger in the same way that Mexicans are familiar strangers in the United States. They speak with an inferior "regional" accent. They belong to the minority religious community of India. In the eyes of some Hindu Bengalis, their religion trumps their ethnolinguistic identity. *Is she Bengali or is she Muslim?* That is the unspoken question hovering in the air. I have heard this question—whispered and shouted out loud—since I was a child living on Dover Lane. *Is she Bengali or is she Muslim? Is he Bengali or is he Muslim?* The answer is predestined. *They have to be one or the other. They cannot be both.* Versions of this very question can be heard all over Europe and America today.

They have to be one or the other. They cannot be both. In that courtroom, I was both. The men whose Bengali I Englished were both. I was American and Bengali. They were Bangladeshi and Bengali. I was Hindu and Bengali. They were Muslim and Bengali. I was a Resident Alien and Bengali. They were undocumented and Bengali. I had skin light enough to pass and was Bengali. They had skin so dark that they could never pass and were Bengali. The court saw me as a solution to their linguistic problems. The court saw them as the ones who caused a problem. I received payment in U.S. dollars for the part I played in court. They were deported out of the country.

When I was a little girl in Calcutta, I had learned to unsee the children who lived behind the garbage dump, the children of the *basti*. Yet, one afternoon, as I lay on the bed pretending to read a book, I had exchanged glances with a boy not much older than me who was squatting on the floor and sweeping it. I knew the space between us was slim enough for me to end up on the floor beside him, sweeping someone else's terrazzo floor. Mine was not a Hollywood fantasy in which a rich man imagines himself swapping places with the poor man as a lark. My terror was darker. I saw us all sliding into the slum hidden behind the rubbish heap.

When I told the men that they had been deported, adjusting my Bengali as best as I could to blunt the sharp edges of the verdict, I looked straight into their eyes across the nondescript courtroom. We needed no language—Bengali or English—to understand that I had been dealt a luckier hand than them that afternoon. Afterward, I rushed out of the building. I could still recall with perfect clarity the morning when I had stood outside the entrance of the U.S. consulate in Calcutta. Only a decade before, I'd had no papers to prove that I was a legal immigrant, the lucky possessor of a green card. If Baba, Ma, and I had not given satisfactory answers (in English) to the man interviewing us, we would have no visas and I would not be standing in a courtroom in America, acting as the official interpreter, relaying a judge's verdict to another Bengali. The space between me and the two defendants was frighteningly narrow.

Going Native was my way of widening the space. Whiteface was my desperate attempt to stay on the right side of a rubbish heap that had followed me across the oceans.

* * *

In 1982, I did not see a black man outside the U.S. consulate located on a street in Calcutta named after Ho Chi Minh. I saw a man whose skin was dark brown in color. His posture was straight. His uniform was spotless. He held his chin up high and looked beyond us into the distance. I do not know if he saw me. And if he did, I wonder what he thought of the Indian family that was trying to immigrate to the United States. Did he see us as *Homo economicus*? Did he think we would steal jobs from native-born Americans? Did he believe that the immigrant's road to becoming American was on the backs of blacks? Did he know that of all the invidious nomenclatures we had invented for each other in Calcutta—Bengali, Non-Bengali, Hindu, Muslim, *bhadralok*, *chhotolok*, vegetarian, non-vegetarian, *bangal*, *ghoti*, touchable, untouchable—racial categories were noticeably absent?

I did not see a black man outside the consulate that day. I saw a man with dark brown skin. The color of his skin was not unusual in Calcutta. There were many people walking around our streets with dark brown skin. I had relatives with dark brown skin. My maternal grandfather's complexion was of a similar color. Some of my great-aunts were even darker. Even his facial features were not new to me. The subcontinent, after all, boasts of a wondrous variety of phenotypes. I have seen Indians with stick-straight hair and the tightest of curls, with thin lips and full ones, with long, sharp noses and wide, broad ones, with narrow and big round eyes that were brown, gray, and even green. So how did I know I had seen a black man outside the U.S. consulate? I had seen a man with skin the color of dark coffee. I had seen a person I presumed was American by virtue of the uniform he wore and position he occupied outside the consulate. That was all I saw.

Until I saw him again in my mind's eye after I landed in

America. I knew then that he was a black man. And in order to see that he was black, I had to perceive the white man—the man who needs no racial adjective, no additional color signifier, no special labels or markings—who forms the backdrop against which a black man is always seen. That second way of seeing was grounded on my tacit understanding of him as Not White. My American education trained me to never name whiteness when I spoke in English. At home, when I spoke in Bengali with my parents, or in Hindi with my husband, we used words such as *shaheb* or *gora*. It was only when I had three children with whom I spoke in English at home did I reconsider naming whiteness. The language I used to name whiteness mattered. Language is no empty vessel. It carries stories, events, emotions from times past. Language always overdelivers. It outstrips its promise. *Blanc. Blank. Blanquito. Caucasian. Farang. Firang. Gora. Sahib. Shaheb. White. Wit.* These words might sometimes point us to the same man standing across the street from us. But they rarely point to the same qualities in the man and the same implicit hopes and fears within the speaker who is gesturing toward the man.

My relationship with English has evolved during the course of the three decades I have spent in the United States. English will always be my third language. It began as the language of school, and flowered into the language of my intellect, while it continued to keep a respectful distance from the language of my emotion. At four, I managed to name a fruit in English and gained entry into an English-medium school. At eleven, I was able to speak English well enough to be interviewed by an employee at the American consulate in Calcutta. At thirteen, I delivered the valedictory speech at the Peabody School in Cambridge. At seventeen, I was admitted to Harvard College with presumably enough fluency in English that no one was concerned about my ability to write papers or follow lectures. At twenty-four, Yale admitted me into the doctoral program in English literature. At twenty-eight, Harvard hired me as an assistant professor of English. What does it mean to be a non-native speaker of English? What does it mean to speak a language as one's third language?

My relationship with English resembles the relationship one has with another human being over the course of a lifetime. Strangers can become intimate friends. Friends can become next of kin. As a child, I did not speak English at home or on the playground. I acquired the language in a school where neither the teachers nor the students spoke English as their first language. I was fluent in English when I was in high school and college. I worried about speaking with the right accent and knowing the correct slang because I did not wish to stand apart as a new immigrant.

What I lacked was a sense of deep intimacy with English. The kind of intimacy with a language that can be found in the whispered lullabies a mother sings to her child at night, that we associate with the nonsense words and silly rhymes used to amuse babies. Miss Solomon taught me how to write English in a pretty cursive hand. American public schools taught me how to forge lifelong friendships in English. American private universities gave me an education in the history, politics, and aesthetics of the English language, from the drunken cowherd Caedmon to Stephen Dedalus's moocow. Every one of these stages deepened my friendship with the language beyond Lord Macaulay's wildest dreams. Yet, other languages—Indian languages—remained the language of my secret heart. Until my children were born.

On official forms I might still be counted as a nonnative speaker of English. I have not abandoned the languages I learned before English. I do not feel estranged from them. I still speak with my parents and my natal family in Bengali. I read magazines and novels in Bengali. I leap at the chance to use my mother tongue when I meet someone from my part of the subcontinent. I enjoy Hindi movies and film songs. I listen almost exclusively to Hindi songs when I am alone in the car. My husband and I switch to Hindi when we wish for a bit of privacy in America. Or when we need quick shorthand for a concept we both grasp better in Hindi. Yet, how can I call English a stranger when it is the sole language with which I love, scold, soothe, and sustain my children? My three children made English the language of my emotions. For them, I had to learn to say new things in English at home, things I had previously said in other languages. For them I had to learn to name whiteness. My children—unable to pass as white because of their complexion, unwilling to pass as white because they belong to a more confident second generation of the immigration story—are of color.

I learned to name whiteness for their sake so that the white officer in front of the consulate door—the man I saw as a *sahib*—did not go unnamed while the other men were made extraordinarily visible with an array of adjectives. A person of color. An Asian man. A Hispanic man. An Indian man. A South Asian man. A black man. A brown man. A yellow man. Having been a young immigrant, I already knew that real power lies in being so dominant that you need not be named. The normal needs no name, no special qualifier. In the United States, there is no need to name the male, the white, the Protestant because these are attributes of the normative. And when we who are not male, white, or Protestant choose to name these things, we risk sounding like people with grievances—angry, shrill, dangerous. We do not need to call the first forty-three presidents of the United States our white presidents or our male presidents or our Christian presidents because that is exactly what all presidents are supposed to be—white, male, Christian. Only divergences need to be pointed out. A Catholic president. A Jewish president. A black president.

A female president. They are a break from the norm. They require the armature of adjectives.

As a college teacher who spent many years lecturing on writings by people from the Caribbean islands, Africa, and the Indian subcontinent, I knew that my students—a diverse group of young people of different races and nationalities—rarely flinched when I named color. We read books by black authors and brown authors. *Black, brown, yellow, orange, red, purple, pink, green.* I could name every color except *white*. If I spoke of *white* ideas, *white* authors, *white* literature, *white* music, *white* aesthetics, *white* politics, or *white* people, then suddenly the atmosphere in the classroom changed. Naming whiteness introduced a note of perceived grievance in my voice. When a person who is Not White names whiteness, ordinary talk turns into race talk. Black, brown, yellow—when we use these colors as descriptors of people, of ideas, of culture we are not shining our light on something that is kept hidden in plain sight. These colors—the people associated with these colors and their actions—are always under scrutiny, in a perpetual state of being vetted.

American life is not unique in this instance. I can find similar patterns in the society in which I was born. In India, *dalit*s, people who are considered untouchable by upper-caste Hindus, are allowed a certain amount of freedom these days by those who consider themselves progressive. Thus, we can talk of *dalit* authors and *dalit* leaders. If, however, an author or a political leader is named as Brahmin, then accusations of fomenting caste warfare rear their heads. The upper-caste is the norm. The lower-caste untouchable exists as departure from, and as inferior to, the norm. Naming the norm robs it of its magic. The equal distribution of adjectives—black and white, man and woman, upper caste and lower caste, rich and poor, Protestant and Catholic—is a potent way of robbing the normative of its invisibility cloak.

I do not want my daughter or my sons to be people of color. I want more for them. I want them to know that they are Not White. I want them to know that their mother, despite her light complexion and despite her semisuccessful attempts at passing when she was younger, is Not White. I want them to know that such a statement, an open declaration of Not Whiteness, once cost people their lives and livelihoods. Today, the same declaration is a rejection of the unspoken code of twenty-first-century American society that hides the derision inherent in "colored people" by rearranging the words into a celebratory "people of color." Not Whiteness dares to name whiteness. It refuses to fly the flag of color while allowing the dominant culture to retain its powerful invisibility. People of Color sings the sweet song of solidarity. It is an affirmation. Not White grunts with belligerence. It is angry. It is a negation. Why would anyone willingly choose a negation over an affirmation for themselves and their children?

The arguments against the belligerence and politics inherent in Not Whiteness are not unfamiliar. Political blackness is no longer fashionable on either side of the Atlantic. The opponents of political blackness argue that Not White erases the differences among people of color; Not White is a disempowering label that makes whiteness the racial equivalent of Greenwich Mean Time; Not White erases the specificity of my Indian heritage, of my exact provenance from one very particular segment of Bengali society. The specifics are important for minorities, especially for second- or third-generation immigrants. Removed from the homeland of their ancestors, my native-born children might one day search for something concrete—the language, the rituals, the music, the dance, the folklore, the vestments of their grandparents. The belligerent grunt that is Not White could sweep those half-forgotten specifics even further away from their grasp.

As a first-generation American I share few of the second and third generations' anxieties. I have forgotten nothing. I still know the old languages. I know how to shape the letters of my mother tongue. I know what to feed a baby during the ceremony of the first solid food. I have not forgotten the stories of the *tuntuni* bird. I have no anxiety of Indianness. Perhaps this is why I feel less of a need to prove my Indianness. I also know that negation carries with it a powerful note of resistance: I am *not* a monotheist. I am *not* Christian. I am *not* European. I am Not White.

I could tell my children that I am a polytheist, a Hindu, an Asian, a person of color. I disown none of these four labels. Yet, I am not satisfied leaving the dominant culture as an unnamed force that shapes the murky meaning of these labels. I grew up worshipping many gods. But no card-carrying polytheist ever calls herself a polytheist. Only a monotheist—someone who believes that one god is superior to many—could invent the idea of polytheism. People have worshipped Shiva for thousands of years in the Indian subcontinent. But Europeans decided to give the name of religion to a complex way of living an ethical life. Asian was a geographic term when I lived in Asia. In the United States, I learned that Asian is a racial category. No one can call themselves a person of color without implicitly seeing their color against a backdrop of whiteness.

For all these reasons and more, I chose Not White. A grunt. A negation. A refusal. A belligerence.

· · ·

I tried to be the good immigrant by assimilating as swiftly as I could when I arrived in the United States as a young girl. I tried to be a grateful immigrant by learning to talk, dress, cook, eat, drink, dance, and even think like an American. Following the logic of meritocracy, I believed that my success was earned by merit. And my merit was my virtue. I was entrepreneurial. I fashioned myself to increase my chances of finding success. I wore whiteface. And just when my colleagues and friends simply "forgot" I was Not White—an unexpected tide of anger welled up inside me. Just when I thought I had succeeded in following the rules of my own DIY whiteface manual, I found myself angry and overwhelmed by sadness.

The angrier I felt, the more I smiled, told jokes, made others laugh so that they would not perceive me as a problem. I took care not to speak Bengali in front of others outside my family. I did not ask for a day off from work when Holi or Durga *puja* or Diwali rolled around. I participated in Christmas festivities with great enthusiasm. In truth, I enjoyed wrapping Christmas presents, surprising colleagues with the perfect Secret Santa gifts, and drinking eggnog. I enjoyed the sharp, clean scent of pine when I stood in the snow, selling Christmas trees for our children's school fund-raisers. Having lost all the festivals of my youth I was eager to mark the seasons in any way possible— Halloween, Thanksgiving, Christmas, Valentine's Day, Easter. There is comfort in rituals that mark the rhythm of each season. And it was also my way of blending into the dominant culture.

I wished to blend into whiteness because I knew how the poor, the foreign, the underclass are only too visible. I knew how the dominant class averts its gaze *and* continues to surveil those who are marked out as different, weak, and dangerous. As a young girl in India, I was trained not to see the things that terrified us—Prakash, the *basti*, the beggars on the streets, the refugees on railway platforms. Our self-inflicted blindness was less a mark of our callousness, and more a sign of our terror. The distance between me and the girls who begged on the streets was so fragile. We did not truly see the maids, cleaners, drivers, and doormen. We did things when our maids were in the room, or when a driver was in the car, that no human normally does in front of another. The master often does not see the slave; the mistress of the house does not see her maid; and I did not see the women who squatted in our kitchen and washed dirty dishes. We did not really see them because they were not quite human to us. So we felt free to carry on as if no one was around.

Our blindness was also an indicator of the outsize importance of the people we chose not see. In Calcutta, Ma and Baba constantly fretted about thieves, kidnappers, and pickpockets. We demonized everyone who came out of that unseen place behind the garbage heap. Today I realize that my blindness was to the *particularity* of the slum dwellers and beggars I saw all around me. I did not see individual human beings. Instead, I saw supersized generalizations. I saw types—*bastibashi, chhotolok, chamar, chheledhora, chor, dakat, jhi-chakor*. These were our words for slum dwellers, lower classes, untouchables, kidnappers, thieves, robbers, servants. Each of these words in Bengali exceeds its dictionary definitions. They are not mere nouns but diffuse, scary ideas used to make a middle-class child obey her elders, ace her exams, and never let go of an adult's hand in a crowd. These words were our own Bengali version of the quintessential American phrase my children have been taught by well-meanings teachers—stranger danger.

Strangers pose danger. I knew that in Calcutta long before I learned this cute English phrase. They can cheat us, rob us, steal us, maim us, and even slit our throats while we sleep in our beds at night. We locked and bolted every door and window at night when we went to sleep. A watchman patrolled Dover Lane and the familiar sound of his bamboo stick hitting the pavement—*thak, thak, thak*—lulled me to sleep. Strangers were dangerous because they could transform us into people like them. We had to remain alert and not look too closely into their eyes.

In New Haven, I was once warned by a fellow student that I had to be careful when walking around town. "Sometimes," this white classmate told me, "you turn a corner and realize you are the only white person walking on the street. Be careful." An awkward pause followed. I walked back to my apartment, muttering to myself about all the things I could have said in response. "I always forget you are Indian," a high school friend told me while we were walking around Harvard Square. She meant it as a compliment. She meant I was not a strange foreigner. That made me even sadder. "But I see you as white," a dear friend confided to me during a work trip to India. We were sitting together on the rooftop of a small house in a Rajasthani village. Perhaps my friend intended to convey that she perceived no difference between us. Perhaps she did not want to see us as separate. In America, separateness is always accompanied by the specter of inequality. Perhaps she wanted to inch away from an America where extraordinary words such as mulatto, quadroon, octoroon, quintroon, terceron, hexadecaroon, mustee, and mustefino were once part of ordinary English. I, who had worked for so long to hide my difference, felt suffocated by the embrace of sameness. Sitting atop an impoverished home in India, looking at the stray dogs, scrawny cows, and mud-caked water buffaloes, with the dusty Aravalli Hills undulating in the distance, I no longer yearned to be seen as white, no matter how pale my skin appeared. I did not wish to leave behind my fellow Indians—even the ones with whom I had few words or foods or gods in common—in their poorly constructed homes, surrounded by heaps of trash and open drains, and disappear into whiteness.

But I see you as white. This is a veiled compliment. The speaker intends to say, "We will let you be on our team. For now. There will be conditions attached in fine print. Ignore them at your own peril." *But I see you as white.* My husband and children have darker brown complexions. My parents' English still carries faint traces of their mother tongue. My Sikh father-in-law wears a turban and has never trimmed his beard. My grandmothers wore saris every day. My aunts carefully placed a red vermilion dot on their foreheads each morning and blew on a conch shell to welcome Durga each autumn. My ancestors were barred from entering European clubs in colonial India, jailed by the British for demanding independence, and designated as terrorists by the British Empire. In the United States, Indian men and women were legally barred from naturalization until the 1940s. *But I see you as white.* Would the same be said of all of them?

I am the kind of Not White that makes human resource managers happy. I blend into whiteness when it is convenient for everyone else in the office. My presence increases diversity when the company is required to present official tallies of minority employees. When we attend conferences, my employers can suggest that I apply for financial aid reserved for minorities in my profession. My Not Whiteness can improve an accountant's bottom line. I am Not Quite Not White. The kind of Not White who makes inclusion look easy and does not make people uncomfortable with her behavior. That is, until someone reads a newspaper article about unemployment in America, or listens to a political speech about the evils of outsourcing, or tunes into a radio program about Asians crowding American universities, or watches a television show about Indians winning the National Spelling Bee yet again. When this happens, I am just Not White enough to become the scapegoat. I am the immigrant who stole the jobs, the minority who gamed the system to snatch away someone else's rightful place in college, the brown person who is unnaturally good at spelling unusually difficult English words.

The smiling member of the model minority can seem uppity in a heartbeat. During our interview at the U.S. consulate in Calcutta, I wish they had told me that I must avoid this sin at all costs if I were to be granted a visa. They should have told me to keep my success within limits, my intelligence in check, and my latent uppitiness under control. I would be at my most pleasing as long as I remained the salutatorian, the runner-up, the solid A minus, the magna cum laude, the Not Quite.

When white people simply "forgot" I was Not White, I did not want to smile any longer. I did not want to be the entertainer. I did not want to be the storyteller who spins a yarn as the earth flows somber under an overcast sky. In Joseph Conrad's *Heart of Darkness*, Charlie Marlow proclaimed that England too was once a place of darkness. I felt very clever when I first detected that line. In a building in Harvard Yard named after a famous American Transcendentalist, I used to teach this very line to my students, pleased with myself for having mastered the literary code of those who once colonized my ancestors. Now, I want that darkness back for myself. I do not wish to accord to white Europeans that which was once used to justify the plunder and conquest of Asia, Africa, and the Americas.

I reclaim the heart of Not Whiteness for myself and my children. Race, once a puzzling, ugly, comic, ill-fitting concept, I realize today, was the immigrant. I chose to make it native to myself. Going against the grain of my education, I decided to naturalize the very concept I once historicized with clinical precision. My Indian past was my way of keeping race at arm's length when I was new to this country. When I became the mother of three children, the future demanded something new of me. The immigrant's story is often written by the second or third generation in America. The American-born child gives birth to the foreign-born parent. Elsewhere is assimilated into the here. The foreign plot is domesticated into the national mythology. Those of the first generation are often too tired, too afraid, too new to English to write their own story. They are busy being good immigrants. When I stopped smiling like a good immigrant, I risked becoming a bad American, an ungrateful immigrant—an angry brown woman. The smile was my road to becoming American. I did not know I would find anger at the end of the journey.

I did not become American by speaking with the right accent, or by dancing to Prince and Salt-N-Pepa, or by eating my steak medium rare and drinking my bourbon neat. Those acts merely Americanized me. And to be *Americanized* is precisely not to be American. I did not become American when I passed the naturalization exam, renounced my Indian citizenship, and swore allegiance to the flag in

Boston's historic Faneuil Hall. I became American by be-coming Not White.

. . .

At the age of ten, I was asked by the Architect to write a letter to the man who was sponsoring Ma, Baba, and me for our visas. I was to write him a letter of thanks for his generosity. The adults around me offered many helpful prompts. I should include a little bit of detail about my life in Calcutta. I should tell him which aspects of American life I anticipated most joyously. I should show him that I had dutifully studied the history of Boston—the city where he lived—and knew the names of its famous landmarks. My letter was to be a demonstration of my worthiness as the young recipient of an American stranger's generosity. Above all, my letter should be written in a neat cursive hand and contain no spelling or grammar errors.

I wrote many drafts of the letter on scrap paper before composing the final fair copy. I had to take out my father's old dictionary to look up two English words: "emigrate" and "immigrate."

Today I looked up those words again in Merriam-Webster's dictionary.

Emigrate—to leave one's place of residence or country to live elsewhere.

Immigrate—to come into a country of which one is not a native for permanent residence.

In order to impress our unseen American benefactor with my knowledge of the English language, I was careful to distinguish between "immigrate" and "emigrate." I wrote that I eagerly anticipated emigrating from India to the United States. When I had arrived in Boston a few years later, and the rules of grammar dictated a change of prefix, I became an immigrant.

Not many native-born Americans I know have opened a dictionary as a child in order to learn the meaning of the word "emigrant." America, after all, is the land of immigrants. A few years ago, when my older son asked me of my first memories of this country, I told him about the bacon smell. "Were you happy, Mama?" my boy, then perhaps nine years old, asked me. He was learning about immigration in his school and the homework assignment was to interview an immigrant. An easy assignment for him since his home was filled with them. No, I wasn't happy, I told him. Suddenly he was on alert.

I noticed that my little interviewer was getting visibly unsettled by the idea that his mother did not experience unmitigated joy when she landed in the country of his birth. In order to soothe my son, I quickly focused on a more upbeat ending. Yes, immigration can be a good news story. I switched to the third person. "Mama made many friends here. She learned to speak like everyone else. She got used to the food. She went to school and got jobs. She began to dream in English. And now she has you and your brother and your sister and your father and she is not lonely anymore. We can all learn to adapt when we move to a new place. And even if we are sad at first, we can eventually be happy. Just like you can be happy if you have to leave this place one day."

"*Whaaaat?* I have to be an immigrant one day?" Clearly my happy ending made my interviewer even more unhappy. "Maybe you will have to go find a job in another country," I replied. "Like where?" asked a scared boy who had been taught that the American immigrant story is heroic and Ellis Island is a cherished landmark.

In the United States, schoolchildren are taught that the American immigrant story has a triumphant ending. The progressive public schools my children attend teach them that we are all immigrants to this land. The uncomfortable question of Native Americans who were already here and Africans who were brought here as slaves is hushed up momentarily. And it is only one sort of immigration that is celebrated. The kind that brings foreigners to these shores. America is the last and final destination. City on a Hill. Promised Land. It is where everyone wants to come. When they come here, they find happiness, equality of opportunity, and freedom. This is how the school textbooks are written.

Why do we only celebrate immigration as an arrival? Emigration is never really contemplated or made a subject in school. I suppose that is the privilege of rich nations—their children are never taught that one day they too might have to go learn a new language, eat new food, become a foreigner somewhere. Should we only teach our children to welcome strangers among us? Or should we also teach them that one day they too might be strangers in a strange land—pushed around the globe by forces of economics, politics, or nature?

Researchers tell us that temporary migrants outnumber permanent migrants worldwide. People do not simply move from one country to another and stay put. Most migrants are seasonal and keep shuttling between two or more places. Where I live in the United States, we focus mostly on permanent migration, and that too in one direction. This, of course, has to do with the historical reality of this country as well as with its foundational myth. Yet, populations have been on the move—in large numbers or small groups, voluntarily or involuntarily (the difference is remarkably difficult to parse, as human rights lawyers will tell us)—since the beginning of human history.

Perhaps my children will wake up one morning in a city halfway across the world to an unfamiliar smell emanating from a kitchen. They might wake up with great joy for having reached a cherished destination. Or they might wake up with a lump in their throat for they have left behind a familiar world. I want them to know that they—like their ancestors before them—will find success and failure, love and disappointment, and eventually go on to welcome other strangers in their new home. Perhaps my children or their children will become part of a new American diaspora. Perhaps they will carry a little bit of America with them wherever they go. Perhaps they will hide it, fearing to be seen as foreign. Perhaps they will nurture the little Americas they carry within them in the privacy of their homes. Perhaps they will teach their descendants of the home they left behind, even as they find themselves inevitably changed from the cousins who remained in the homeland.

Wherever you must go one day, I told my son who wanted to celebrate his immigrant parents and yet remained fearful of emigration himself, you will always remember how quiet it suddenly gets before a big snowstorm arrives, how the lily of the valley in our front yard always blooms around the first week of May, how maple syrup tastes when you pour it on warm pancakes, how nice it feels to hear the basketball players across our street on a hot summer night, how I told you and your brother and your sister the story of Hutum the owl each night at bedtime, how happy you felt during the car ride to New Hampshire the day we picked up our new puppy, how you must tell your teacher the correct way to pronounce your name at the beginning of each school year, how you were once ashamed to call us Mama and Baba in front of your classmates and insisted on calling us Mom and Dad, and how you outgrew your shame.

We have truly arrived when we are no longer afraid of departure. The emigrant once anticipated America. The new *arrivant* attempted to assimilate, donning whiteface and a wide smile. The American—with no further need for Americanization—knows that we carry our household gods, our Lares, within ourselves wherever we roam.

·   ·   ·

Did I really see a black man outside the U.S. consulate in Calcutta all those years ago? No, I did not see a black man outside the consulate, because I did not see race. I did not get race until I arrived in the United States. And when I did get race in all its many American incarnations—defined variously and contradictorily through genetics, linguistics, geography, and even, on occasion, through theology— I saw the man outside the consulate anew. Black is a color. Black is a history. Black is a politics. Black is a story. Black is a memory. Black is an emotion. Black is a language. Brown is a color. Brown is a history. Brown is a politics. Brown is a story. Brown is a memory. Brown is an emotion. Brown is a language. And so is white. White is a color. White is a history. White is a politics. White is a story. White is a memory. White is an emotion. White is a language.

Within the heart of Not Whiteness lies the power to name whiteness. By naming whiteness, I do not grant it more centrality or power. I give it shape and local habitation. I make it come down from its high perch of normativity and assume its rightful place among all the other colors. I contain it and domesticate it before it can contain and domesticate me and my children. I refuse to grant it the magic power of invisibility. I make it less free to move about without being stopped and frisked, without passports and visas. By naming whiteness, I do not allow it to lay sole claim to all that we choose to call American.

Once I thought that to be Americanized was to pass as white. Now I am American because I know I am Not White. The knowledge makes me grin.

ACKNOWLEDGMENTS

The goddess of knowledge has a vast domain. Her flowers are enchanted. Miss Solomon and Hriday Singh. Jamuna, Mundi, and Prakash. All my teachers at the Pilot School in Cambridge. Sara Suleri Goodyear, Vera Kutzinski, Noelle Morrissette, Romita Ray, and Joseph Thompson. Homi Bhabha, Eileen Chow, Susan Donnelly, Lynn Festa, Henry Louis Gates, Jr., Maya Jasanoff, Robert Orsi, Michael Puett, Sunil Sharma, and Helen Vendler. George Lucas, Sheila Moody, Oliver Munday, Elda Rotor, and Elizabeth Vogt. Gabriella Coniglio and C. Y. Lung. Ruchira Sen and Prabodh Chandra Sen. Chitra Banerji and Shantanu Kumar Banerji. Aparna Sen and Silabhadra Sen. Satwant Singh and Ajit Singh. Annmarie Charles. Rupinder Singh, Ishani Singh, Milan Singh, and Kabir Singh. And Atticus. You are present on each page of this book. In each pressed, pale orange marigold petal.